WITH SAVIOR

MESSAGES FROM SPACE BEING YAIDRON

HS PRESS

With Savior

Messages from Space Being Yaidron

Ryuho Okawa

HS Press

Original title: *With Savior Kyuseishu to Tomoni*
-Uchu Sonzai Yaidron no Message-
HS Press is an imprint of IRH Press Co., Ltd.
Tokyo
ISBN 13: 978-1-943869-94-7
ISBN 10: 1-943869-94-4

The opinions of the space being in this book do not necessarily reflect those of Happy Science Group.
For the mechanism behind spiritual messages, see the end section.

Contents

CHAPTER TWO

Earthlings Viewed from the Universe

Spiritual Messages from Yaidron

In this book, there are a total of three interviewers from Happy Science, symbolized as A, B, and C, in the order that they first appear.

Preface

You may find this a mysterious book.

A person with interest will enjoy it thinking, "How generous to have revealed secrets this much," while a person with no interest will make a grimace and say, "Well, he can say whatever he wants."

Space being Yaidron has given a message.

He and also Metatron and R. A. Goal are the space beings that are closest to me and are constantly around protecting me from their UFO or mother ship.

You will know why if you read the book, *Daichukateikoku Houkai eno Jyokyoku* (literally, "The Prelude to the Collapse of the Great Chinese Empire") (Tokyo: IRH Press, 2020). There are spiritual beings with evil intentions that are trying to stop my activities, and sometimes, the power of the terrestrial assisting spirits alone is not enough.

Some of you may say, "You want me to believe in space people when I can't even believe in ghosts?" But remember, it was this year that the U.S. President Donald Trump publicly admitted the existence of

UFO and space beings. The truth can no longer remain hidden.

Ryuho Okawa
Master & CEO of Happy Science Group
August 30, 2020

CHAPTER ONE

With Savior

Messages from Space Being Yaidron

Originally recorded in Japanese on August 23, 2020, in the Special Lecture Hall of Happy Science in Japan, and later translated into English.

Yaidron

A space being from Planet Elder in the Magellanic Clouds. He is a powerful being with higher-dimensional powers in the Earth Spirit World and is a god of justice-like being. On Elder, he works as someone like the chief justice and highest-ranking statesman and is in charge of justice and judgment. In the past, Yaidron was taught by El Cantare on a Messiah-training planet and is currently protecting Master Ryuho Okawa, who is the human incarnation of El Cantare. Yaidron has an infinite life span, transcending both physical and spiritual bodies. He has been involved with the rise and fall of civilizations, wars, and major disasters on Earth.

A video footage of Yaidron's UFO was recorded on Sept. 28, 2020. You can search "Yaidron UFO" on YouTube or go to the link below to watch it:
https://youtu.be/FR_1Y0kuWJY

1

Messages from "Space Guardian" Yaidron

RYUHO OKAWA

Good morning. Today, I would like to do a spiritual message that is a little different from the usual ones. I am thinking of receiving a message from the space being Mr. Yaidron, an individual who we owe a lot to.[1]

We received multiple messages from outer space before the coronavirus outbreak, but now, more than six months have passed. We are now headed toward the end of August, so I believe he may have different thoughts or feelings about the future.

We have received many opinions from Mr. Yaidron, but he tends to work in the background and would come when things are getting out of hand, or when we are annoyed, and give us suggestions. So, we do not have many official spiritual messages from him. We do not have many official video recordings of his messages.

Today's title is, "With Savior." Ever since Governor Koike of Tokyo started using the phrase "With corona (virus)," many things happened using the phrase "The age of 'with corona'," though I feel this is not very good English.

So, I would like Mr. Yaidron to talk about a different phrase, "With Savior." He is like our guardian deity, so I think he always has this kind of thought in his mind. Also, his appearance is still hidden, so I believe that historically, human beings received the voices of existences like him, not just inspirations from high spirits in the heavenly world.

He can determine things that spirits who are from Earth cannot speak of, in an objective, calm way and with detail, so it should be helpful. So, we would appreciate it if he can speak of things that we would not realize.

Usually, he appears with our UFO photos or footage. However, today, we would like to stay away from that. Since we are not a professional media, I am not sure how skillful you are at asking the right questions. You may be scolded for asking questions that are too much based on the Earthlings' way of thinking.

Anyway, I will call him because now, he seems to have things to say about the future. Let us hear Mr. Yaidron's messages from outer space.

Mr. Yaidron, Mr. Yaidron.

Please deliver your voice to Happy Science and through us, convey the message you would like to share with people who are interested. Thank you very much.

[*About 10 seconds of silence.*]

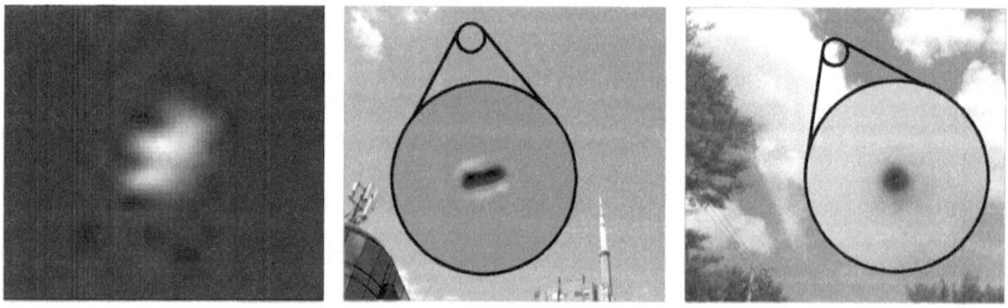

A few of the photos and videos of Yaidron's UFO captured up to now. From left: September 24, 2018 in Japan (video), October 4, 2019 in Toronto, Canada (photo), and July 2, 2020 in Japan (photo).

2
Yaidron's Thoughts on the Coronavirus Problem

The novel coronavirus is not a spontaneous occurrence

YAIDRON
This is Yaidron.

A
Good morning. Thank you very much for today.

YAIDRON
Yes.

A
This year, 2020, is said to be the turning point for the future and of the civilization. It was predicted from the end of last year that something extremely big will happen. First, the coronavirus issue hit the whole globe. That is also an issue concerning China. And, the battle

for hegemony between the United States and China is getting intense.

The first thing people are concerned about is what will happen with the coronavirus and the future of humanity. We would appreciate it if you can talk about the outlook on this topic.

YAIDRON

From our perspective, it looks like the Earthlings have become mentally unstable and are trying to commit mass suicide.

The coronavirus that spread throughout the world is not a spontaneous occurrence, according to our analysis. It seems like some people are emphasizing that it was a natural occurrence that happened spontaneously in order to avoid taking responsibility, but it was nothing like that.

We think it was developed by some humans in order to spread the illness to other humans and lead them to death. Our thoughts are unwavering on this.

Many spirits seem to be saying something similar in your spiritual messages, but people in this world are trying to manipulate information and confuse others by saying the virus happened spontaneously or that it happened in multiple countries at the same time. This is all because these people want to evade responsibility. The virus was engineered and disseminated with a clear intention to bring about a global crisis.

The development of vaccines will not immediately end this pandemic

YAIDRON

The result is yet to come, since this is a matter taking place in real time. At this time, the official number of infected people is over 20 million. When the first spiritual messages on this issue came out, the number was only around 10,000 or 20,000 or 30,000, but now, it is over 20 million, and considering there are many that have not been tested, it should be much higher in reality. It is only a matter of time when this number will reach 100 million.

Fortunately, the fatality rate is nowhere close to 50 percent, so people can recover. I heard that many who have died had some kind of disability or were of an older age.

Currently, many places are working to develop vaccines, but as the virus moves through various ethnic groups, humans are developing resistance or immunity toward the virus, so the virus itself is continuously mutating little by little as well to defeat that. Therefore, the development of vaccines may not immediately end this pandemic.

I think that when these things spread rapidly, it is important to consider why it became rampant. Of course, the ones who deliberately spread it are responsible, but the ones affected must also consider what issues there are on a global scale.

What will happen from the second wave on?

YAIDRON

If you would like to know in detail, please ask me more about that.

A

Before we go into that, the immediate concern people have is how big the second wave will be and how badly it will affect the world. The current fatality rate has dropped compared to the beginning, so the damage is not that big.

Would the virus become ferocious again or not, and if it would, how big would the problem be? These are the questions in concern. What do you think?

YAIDRON

You know, [*sighs*]... In reality, I think we have passed World War III and entered into World War IV. Originally, it was expected that World War III would involve mass murder using nuclear weapons. Nuclear weapons still exist, but it is difficult for any country to play a one-sided game since we can tell who used the weapons if someone uses them, and it would invite a counterattack and would cause significant damage to themselves.

However, in a viral attack, the suspect is not apparent or the perpetrator cannot be identified. So, although nuclear weapons are still an option, it is certain that there are people who thought of putting the world into chaos using the virus first.

The damage is especially heavy in the U.S., Brazil, Europe, and India. So, yes... the perpetrator is testing the virus without leaving traces behind. I think so.

As for your question of what will happen from the second wave on, hmm... If the perpetrator does not acknowledge what they did, it is possible that the affected side may do something similar to attack them.

It is very difficult to gain consensus to wage a hot war against the perpetrator of the virus attack when the party responsible cannot be determined accurately. Next, another country could possibly launch this kind of viral war. In that case, everything will become vague and it is unclear how far it will go.

Anyway, humanity has reached a population of about 7.8 billion and I believe everyone is sensing that there will be problems of food and energy if this number continues to increase.

Everyone may want only their own nation to survive, but that is not acceptable. Many things may happen hereafter that will decrease the world population. These issues are never transparent and tend to be considered in secrecy.

The biggest shock this time was that the world's number one city, New York, suffered the greatest damage. The biggest since the Islamic terrorist attack. The world was trying to become stronger by cooperating with each other, but when something like the coronavirus spreads... For example, something like the EU, where dozens of nations come together to connect beyond borders, may seem like a way that will generally increase economic strength, but it becomes very weak to the virus attack because it cannot close its borders.

This is what is happening. Mutual suspicion arises among humanity and the situation is making people keep a distance from each other. This is a value that is the opposite of what we have had. It is as if to say, "If you love someone, distance yourself." I believe a reversal of values is about to happen.

What Yaidron means by "human beings want to commit mass suicide"

YAIDRON

Japan, I believe, is quite behind in this sense.

However, 25 years ago, an evil new religious cult committed a terrorist attack using poisonous gas and this had a great impact on the world. It showed that a group can commit a sarin gas attack or a biological weapons attack if they have sufficient funds.

Attacks using these chemical or biological weapons are called the pauper's nuclear weapon. The world is keeping a close watch on nuclear development today, but such a style of attack can sneak through the eyes of the world. Poisonous gas has already been used in Syria as well. If poisonous gas and viral attacks begin to be used, the situation would get out of control.

In this sense, as I said in the beginning, I feel that human beings want to commit mass suicide. That is why I think it is necessary to spread new values. The basis behind the current situation is that humans are thinking only of survival in this world. If people think only of survival in this world, they end up only considering the continuation of their own race or nation, just like how past religious wars happened. Some people think in this way.

So, what will happen during the second wave is a bit difficult to grasp as the second wave, third wave, and many other things will happen. Aside from this, there are floods, swarms of locusts, heat waves, and many other phenomena. I believe there are many people who cannot understand why those are happening.

Japanese people may not know, but there are places that research how to create typhoons or cyclones that can create gigantic damage, so eventually, it may become hard to determine whether the occurrence is natural or not.

In any case, I can say that if someone is free to consider several possible ways to decrease the population of 7.8 billion to, for example, about five billion, many of them may be realized. That is what lies from the second wave on.

3

The Savior Appears in Times of Crisis

Humankind is now being asked to get back on the right track

A

The coronavirus issue is thought to have occurred through artificial means. Under the current situation, does the heavenly will intend to make other natural disasters or something like that happen, as a way to decrease the population to five billion?

YAIDRON

Life in this world, as you all are already exploring, is provided as experiment ground for the soul existences of the Real World to live in a physical body, and as a classroom for study, so we are always examining if it is an environment worthy of that. When it was unworthy, sometimes the civilization ended or the whole continent sank.

As a step before that, there are examples of human-initiated crises, such as people from an advanced civilization annihilating a less advanced ethnic group. For example, Spanish people went to South America and eradicated the civilization of the local race, a civilization centered on the king. There were also cases where European countries colonized India and other Asian nations.

There have been incidents of degrading certain ethnic groups into the slave class. The issue involving the Jewish people that continues to this day comes from the problem of their being once slaves in Egypt. Sometimes things of this level occur.

Also, it may not be worth pointing out anymore, but there were outbreaks of new diseases in the past such as the Black Death during the medieval times or smallpox or other diseases in ancient times. I believe it was not possible for people back then to determine the cause of these diseases.

In times when transportation methods were limited, diseases to which people who lived in certain areas were immune were not the case for other ethnic groups, so the spread of such disease caused a decrease in population. For example, the Black Death happened when religious wars were at their peak. It happened when the Islamic regions and Christian regions were fighting fiercely and also when the Catholics and Protestants within Christianity were fighting harshly. These are cases where illness from a nation was brought to another nation when different nations clashed in a form of war.

What lies behind this has not been clarified entirely, but there are cases where a whole ethnic group or nation is eradicated. There are many cases like this in history. The current virus war has not yet reached the final stage because the final stage would be the extinction of civilization. So, there are still several steps until that point.

I believe we can think that in the meantime, humanity is being requested to get back on the right track.

It is in times of crisis that a savior appears and the will of the universe is revealed

B

Thank you very much for today. Regarding what you mentioned earlier about how the Earth is moving toward mass suicide, it may appear as a battle of earthly values among Earthlings, to space beings like you, Mr. Yaidron.

As in the title "With Savior," given for today's session, when I think of the will of existences like the savior, I feel that the Earth has deviated much more from the way it should be. If you were to consider the whole Earth as a single human being, it is probably in a state where it cannot reflect on itself.

Could you give us some hints on what we as Earthlings should do in order to stop ourselves from heading toward mass suicide?

YAIDRON

From our perspective, we are not allowed to interfere in Earth's civilization in times of peace, so we are just observing the people of Earth doing things as they wish. However, there is an exceptional provision that says we can interfere when a big problem occurs that makes it difficult for humans to continue to exist. In a sense, this condition gives us the opportunity to show ourselves, give our opinions, and change the direction of humanity.

You were told that the Golden Age starts in 2020. You may think, "How could it be the Golden Age when many bad things are happening globally?" From our point of view, though, we have now been given the opportunity to be fully involved with Earth and it is our chance to convey to the ignorant and stubborn Earthlings what the beings of space civilizations are thinking, or how the will of the universe works. So, it is a crisis for humankind, but the savior appears because it is a crisis, and this is also when the will of the universe is revealed.

In this sense, an opportunity for change is being given to this planet, which has been managed only by the ideas of the people of Earth. We are trying to teach them that their way of thinking is at a roadblock, and that if there are conflicts among the ideas they themselves created and they are unable to resolve the conflict, an outside power can begin to work.

The current virus in question is, in short, the "communist virus." The virus called communism began to spread throughout the Earth from the latter 1800s and it has fought its way into various places on the planet. From another perspective, you are facing a situation in which the "communist party virus" or the "communism virus" is spreading, trying to devour the "Faith DNA," or the people who believe in God. It is trying to devour those who have the "DNA to believe in God," so clearly, a stage is currently being set where we must somehow detoxify or extinguish this communist party virus.

Humankind is being watched to see at what point they will call the name of God

C

Would the method to detoxify or extinguish this communism virus or communist party virus which you just mentioned, ultimately be a war of thoughts?

YAIDRON

Basically, I think it is about making people feel the existence of God, so mystical phenomena or miracles that make people feel the presence of God must happen and higher dimensional ways of thinking or thoughts must be conveyed from advanced beings. In this sense, the doomsday phenomena which may not have happened enough in the 20th century are coming a little later, in the 21st century. Humankind must fight against these and the result will change depending on what values and thoughts they will choose. Regarding this, there will be a conflict of free will between humans.

Currently, a savior has appeared and is delivering his opinion, but it has not yet reached the point of detoxifying or eradicating the evil ideological virus in the world. If you have accurate knowledge, you will clearly know that the ideas of materialism, atheism, and agnosticism are all wrong from the perspective of the savior or those of us who are giving power to the savior. But if humans cannot accept this, all kinds of disasters will occur.

I think humans are being watched to see at what point they will call the name of God.

4
The Battle against "Knowledge Communism" Has Begun

The three battles that await materialist China

A

The U.S.-China war is about to break out as a battle against the Communist Party and materialism. However, the structure is not as simple since America is not completely a country of faith either, and we are worried about this current situation.

If you look at the United States itself, you can see that it is beginning to resemble China in some ways. President Trump's opinion has been completely blocked by the media and his speech is practically suppressed. The Democratic Party is strongly left-wing and their vice presidential candidate seems to think in a communist fashion. So, even if the United States wins, I do not think humans will rid themselves of their materialistic and atheistic arrogance.

Even if the truly dangerous totalitarian people are removed, materialism will remain, and a part of humanity is moving toward that. I would appreciate it if you could teach us about what will happen or what is necessary for humanity to shift toward belief in God.

YAIDRON

From a global perspective, there is a tendency for people from poorer regions to have stronger faith and once the economic level rises and the value of each human becomes higher, the faith begins to decline. There is a tendency that, although faith spreads in poor nations, wealthier ones forget God and Buddha and see themselves as gods. The exception is the United States in which the people's level of faith is high despite how the economic level rose. So, there is still hope.

Also, as the power after China, I think India is drawing close. It is probably not very easy to turn India into an atheist nation. The 1.2 or 1.3 billion citizens have quite strong faith even though they have many tens of different faiths. So, if the U.S., with its Christian faith based standpoint, cannot win against the materialist ideology, next there will surely be a battle between that ideology and the Indian values.

There is also the issue of what will become of the Islamic areas because Islam has spread quite widely to poor regions. It has spread from the Middle East to Africa and in some areas, a handful of people like royalties are extremely prosperous from oilfield rights. So, a communist revolution may extremely readily take place there. However, even if the people carry out a communist revolution, there is the question of whether they will dismiss God or not. Therefore, the Chinese values will also face such battle against the forces of Islam.

In this sense, looking at the human civilization, the materialist and atheist nation will not be able to establish a global empire unless they overcome the three battles, "the battle against the American civilization," "the battle against the Indian civilization," and "the battle against the Islamic civilization."

Protecting the Earth as a place for soul learning is a must

YAIDRON

We are now watching over these three battles. We have the mission of giving people an opportunity to awaken by sending out some kind of opinion or phenomenon if necessary.

So, there are many different types of beings coming to Earth now from the universe. Currently, Earth's civilization is at a turning point and there are many beings coming to observe it. It is not just one type. Numerous types of beings from highly civilized planets that are more advanced than Earth are coming to this planet and looking at humans as if to look at the animals from the outside, just like at the Ueno Zoo. Some of them, like us, are starting to intervene by contacting people.

The ways of thinking in the universe have some differences in opinion too, so it is necessary to reconcile these thoughts. There is quite a lot of differences between planets, so they do understand the reason why opinions differ among people of Earth according to race and nation. Still, there is a common term in ways of thinking, so I believe it is necessary for us to lay out this guideline.

At the least, protecting the Earth as a place for soul learning is an absolute must. From a greater perspective, people are not only going through the soul reincarnation experiment solely on Earth. From time to time, on the universe level, human-like beings from other planets are born as humans on Earth, and humans that lived on Earth gain new experience by reincarnating on another planet. I am not sure if the present people on Earth can understand to this extent, but such a world exists as the truth of the universe, so whether Earthlings can understand this or not, we must preserve a certain level of environment for soul learning.

Therefore, if the Earth enters a difficult era where a thermonuclear war breaks out and mass genocide happens, we will not hesitate to intervene using military means. We have the power to extinguish all the nuclear weapons on Earth within a week. Although we have this power, if possible, I wish for people of Earth to make these judgments with their own free will and sense of responsibility.

One such means is for a savior to appear and preach the teachings through the doomsday phenomena and present the direction humanity should proceed toward, and the test is whether the multitude of people will follow or not.

Knowledge is becoming the source of authority in the present era

A

According to what you just mentioned, the materialist nation not only needs to win against the United States but also India and Islam. You taught us there are multiple scenarios, but can you tell us the most probable scenario regarding the ongoing conflict between the U.S. and China?

YAIDRON

There is another problem. The communist way of thinking originally comes from the issue of distribution of wealth in the material sense, which became the issue of debate. People thought of what to do with the difference among the wealthy and poor, or that the poor are being exploited. The communist idea was conceived to balance this and realize equality through redistribution.

This was already an issue in the aristocracy that continued from the Middle Ages to the modern era. Aristocracy made a portion of the people wealthy and the commoners remained suffering, which led to the idea that if they destroy aristocracy and redistribute the wealth, everyone's level of living would improve. This is how people may usually think. This itself is something we can understand. Especially under imperial rule, where an awful king makes the people suffer for a long time by not governing well, for example, frequently executing them or crushing those who are rebellious, such revolution had to be accepted to a certain extent.

However, the problem today is not just disparity in wealth, but the fact that the communist way of thinking can be seen regarding knowledge. Since the one that has more knowledge gains the upper hand, we can now see status disparity due to education and the rule of media over humankind through monopoly and oligopoly of knowledge starting to occur.

In this sense, for example within the United States, aside from the battle between the Republican and Democratic Parties, many people are becoming able to gain knowledge even though they are not nobility or royalty, and their knowledge is turning into the source of authority. From an era where wealth was the source of authority, we are entering an era where knowledge is becoming the source of authority. There has been the problem of inequality from maldistribution of wealth, and now there is a problem of maldistribution of knowledge, meaning the one who has the authority to gather and use knowledge may become the greatest power within the democratic system. These two problems are happening simultaneously.

This kind of civilization project is going on in the United States and the president must fight as an individual against the numerous powers that have knowledge.

Tyrannical selection and forcing of knowledge in countries such as China

YAIDRON

On the other hand, in countries like China, they have knowledge but people are brainwashed or restricted in access to knowledge based on a certain value judgment. In short, the present administration does not allow people to use knowledge in a way that opposes the ruler. The administration backed by military power is executing its authority and ordering its people to robotize.

(As reported) In today's news, it said the history textbooks used in Hong Kong will voluntarily refrain from writing about the Tiananmen Square Incident, meaning that there is pressure to pretend it never happened. So, they are deleting those things on their own. They are pretending that things inconvenient for them did not happen. Inconvenient damage never occurred.

Therefore, if the government announced that, "After Xi Jinping entered Wuhan, there have been no Chinese virus-infected persons or deaths, and the only exceptions were small numbers of cases that were from facilities that accepted the Chinese people who returned from foreign countries, so China has succeeded in completely suppressing the virus," people cannot object to it.

The dictatorial force that communism should be fighting to take down, is actually being born within communism itself. An authority that chooses and forces knowledge on others has appeared.

In the United States, the law of the jungle over knowledge power is happening within a free market, but in China, which is not a free society, tyrannical selection and forcing of knowledge are taking place.

Currently, knowledge is becoming a power and has come to the point where it is suppressing human rights and depriving human life. In the past, wealth was the enemy, but now, it's not only that; knowledge is becoming an issue too.

The next revolution is a battle against the monopoly of knowledge

YAIDRON

This Chinese influence has also infiltrated into Japan, and the American intelligent leftists' "knowledge is almighty" idea has seeped deeply into Japan's academics and the world of media. The underlying tone is practically, atheism, materialism, agnosticism, and scientism.

Therefore, the next revolution will not only be a battle against the monopoly of wealth and power by the king and nobility. We will need to consider how to weaken the power of those who are monopolizing knowledge and controlling it. That is why we are sending out things that people who are monopolizing knowledge do not have, as messages from this religion or space beings, to nullify their power.

President Trump cited three examples from the Pentagon's records as proof that UFOs are coming to Earth. For the first time as president, he officially disclosed that unidentified flying objects possibly with extraterrestrial beings are coming to Earth. He has more information, so he might come out with those, and this is how he is trying to drill a hole into whatever is controlling the people through the monopoly of knowledge.

He is receiving inspiration from the higher realms of Earth's Spirit World, but he is also beginning to open up the hidden fact that former U.S. presidents have been delivered with certain messages from the universe. That is how today's "knowledge communism" may be defeated.

The mass media, etc., which monopolizes knowledge, are not necessarily on the side of the people anymore; instead, they are preying on the people. They are now a class that controls citizens for the purpose of collecting subscription or viewing fees. That class can control the people, and at the same time, it is becoming a power that can defang powerful figures and make them its puppets.

Messages from space people will leave the media powerless

YAIDRON

The president of the United States is using Twitter as a tool to release his opinion, since the media cannot control it. But even though a president uses it to give his opinion, what he says can be deleted based on how Twitter thinks. So, here exists another terrible authority.

They will not allow you to speak freely. You cannot freely deliver your words. You cannot deliver them without going through another entity. So, there is another battle aside from one between the disparity and distribution of wealth—one between the collection and distribution of knowledge.

In response to this, we are trying to leave them powerless by throwing in other-dimensional, unknown knowledge. The same goes for this message, "With Savior." Not "With Coronavirus" because the coronavirus does not talk. Releasing a message from space people with the title "With Savior" is a powerful and mind-wrecking punch for newspapers and TV.

The fact that there are subjects that they cannot get information from or cannot interview means they have a weakness. If there is a person who can obtain information from those subjects that they cannot interview, it means that such media authority is no longer as firm as a rock. If, for example, we could draw a scenario of the battle between the United States and China, it would be fearful for the people of Earth. But of course, we do plan to make people choose by themselves as much as possible.

5
Forecasting How the U.S.-China Conflict and U.S. Presidential Election Will Unfold

"I am trying to bring about a reform from within China"

YAIDRON

But there are many battles China must fight before it can establish hegemony. Aside from the coronavirus, it is facing many crises and becoming increasingly isolated from the world.

In terms of forming alliances... Former communist state Russia would rather get back into the G8. Iran is in a very weakened state right now because of the economic sanctions. China is trying to reach out to India's rival Pakistan and Mr. Xi Jinping is trying to go to South Korea, but this indicates that they are feeling the pinch right now.

Recently, the Chinese premier let slip how much the Chinese citizen's average annual income is. Base your calculations on that and you will know China's true GDP. He said there are about 600 million people whose monthly income is about ¥15,000 (about $140), for example. Those who are well-off and not considered a part of that group also have a very low annual income that is around ¥450,000 (about $4,200). Calculate that by the number of the national population and, assuming that the numbers are correct, the entire GDP of China would be only ¥630 trillion (about $5.9 trillion).

Japan's GDP is over ¥500 trillion (about $4.7 trillion). That might go down because of the coronavirus, but in either case, this reveals that their claim that "China surpassed Japan's GDP a long time ago. It is now double its size and is about to surpass the U.S." is an utter lie. This is being leaked out by the premier. Xi Jinping is trying to create an empire based on lies. This is being leaked out from within.

If the communist party says "seven percent growth," then it is made so. The country claims to have grown by seven percent every year. They publish their performance figures, but in reality, the people are poor. Any politician who has some sense of justice will look at this contradiction and naturally think, "This must be corrected at some point."

Our focus right now is centered on bringing about a force that will rise together with Hong Kong and Taiwan in their resistance to the Beijing government. To that end, we are causing the floods, the damage from the locusts, and many other crises such as food shortages or being isolated through economic sanctions by other countries and losing foreign friends. In this way, we are trying to get them to reform from within.

China and South Korea, who are both disliked, are now trying to get close to each other again, but that is because they are isolated from other countries in the world. Their way of thinking is out of touch with the rest of the world.

When these internal affairs are brought out into the open, these nations will collapse, just as the Soviet Union did.

The kind of thinking that befits the president of the United States

A

You spoke about how China will collapse from within.

One matter of immediate concern to us is the U.S. presidential election. We believe this will be the turning point to determine the near future. Objectively, the situation seems very tough for Mr. Trump. What do you think are the chances of him winning?

YAIDRON

Hmm... [*About 10 seconds of silence*].

People in the movie business on the West Coast and those in New York where the coronavirus was widespread have a very left-wing way of thinking. Areas representative of the U.S. are now anti-Trump. There is also a trend to ridicule anything Trump-like by calling it "anti-intellectual."

The fact is, even among American politicians, there are too many who have never been anything but a politician. They cannot see how the public finances for an entire nation must be administered.

Also, how much the Obama Administration had made the U.S. poorer and was, in fact, unable to save the poor is covered up. How much they allowed China to become a more evil country is also covered up. The mass media has not shared official information about these.

This is indeed a big battle. But, so far, we are working toward getting Mr. Trump reelected. We are also thinking to select someone who holds a similar way of thinking as the next person after Trump.

What we look for when making our choice is, someone who can increase America's national strength and also explicitly declare their faith in God. We believe that it is better that such a person becomes president. We cannot support someone who has the opposite way of thinking. I believe it will be very hard for Mr. Biden to become president, and should he become president, there will certainly be some repercussions. I believe it will accelerate the fall of America.

The reason comes down to this. Mr. Biden simply does not understand what Mr. Trump has done in the past three and a half years. He (Mr. Trump) has the eyes of a company executive, so he knows how to make

America prosper. Mr. Biden, however, continues to think he can tax the big corporations and distribute it to the poor. His way of thinking is closer to communism or that of a social welfare state. He is not thinking in the direction that will increase the wealth of America. I believe he will inherit the mismanagement of the Obama era.

Electing Biden will lead to the emergence of a second Hitler

YAIDRON
As much as I am allowed to intervene from outer space, I want to strengthen the current administration and the one who will follow it, but intellectuals in Japan and in the U.S. regard Mr. Trump as a "divider." They think he will isolate the U.S. from the world and the world will fall apart. But, in reality, electing Mr. Biden will result in an appeasement policy (toward China) which will lead to the emergence of a second Hitler.

I do not wish the American people to be so foolish to allow that. If Mr. Biden and the one who will follow after him—whether that will be the vice president or someone else, I do not know—take office, the U.S. will distance themselves further and further from China and isolate themselves instead.

Objectively, this will mean that the U.S. admits to losing the virus war. It will mean that they lost to the virus war China waged on them. Because the damage they suffered not only in the U.S. but across North America and South America was so great, they will think, "Far from Jupiter, far from his thunder," and stay clear of China. Out of fear, they will cease to speak out against China. Then, China will no longer hide their desire to take over the United Nations and dominate the world.

In response, the smaller nations of Asia will begin their resistance. In the EU, it will be a matter of how much they will let China buy them out. In Africa, it will be a matter of how much it is taken over. A great hegemonism will begin.

To avert this, we have already begun to bring acts of God or natural disasters upon China, so that it will not go in that direction. But there is much more we are thinking of doing. We have plans in place, so that Xi Jinping cannot become emperor for life.

China's reform will be brought about by countless revolutionaries and heroes

C

You spoke of people inside China who respond to your way of thinking. Could you elaborate on this more? You said that in a U.S. president, you look for the ability to increase America's national strength and also explicitly declare their faith in God. What are the qualities you require in the people who will remove Xi Jinping from power and stand as leaders of China?

YAIDRON

I believe that, despite the countless oppression by the police and military, there will be a people's uprising first. That is because, without the people's backing, reform will not be possible.

China is becoming increasingly isolated from the international community mainly due to the Hong

Kong issue. There are intellectuals in China, and especially those who have returned from living abroad have a fairly accurate understanding of what exactly is happening. In contrast, it is people like Mr. Xi Jinping who do not understand. They really think they, a single country, are running the world.

There will indeed be the rise of revolutionaries. There are about... 90 million communist party members, but about 80 percent of them feel a sense of distrust toward the current administration. When the fact that about 80 percent of these people harbor distrust comes to the fore as actual numbers, when the truth becomes apparent that China is not progressing economically, that poverty is only accelerating, and that they are poorer even compared to other countries, or when Mr. Xi Jinping further causes China to become increasingly isolated because he is unlearned in international diplomacy, a great surge for reform will rise from within. A revolt will also occur from the media companies that are tightly government-controlled. And, there will be people who will break through the censorship placed on the Internet by intelligence agencies and intelligence police and try to get the information out.

It will not be an individual, but it will be countless revolutionaries or heroes who will do so. It will not be specific individuals.

6

The Road to Rebuilding Humanity

Japan has no one to fall back on to steer itself

A

Thank you.

We heard from you about the state of international affairs. On another note, regarding Japan, there are concerns about Prime Minister Abe's health (On August 28, 2020, Prime Minister Abe expressed his will to resign as prime minister due to his chronic illness). Domestically, he has fumbled the coronavirus issue and his leadership ability has diminished considerably. We would like to hear it if you have an opinion on how Japan should steer itself forward.

YAIDRON

Japan pretty much doesn't have anyone to fall back on to steer it. The doings of the present administration were done with the approval of Japan's main media companies. This means that the power behind-the-scenes is the media. If the media allows for a tax increase, then the government can move forward with it. This is what the state of Japan has become. The limit of the media's intellect now determines the limit of Japanese politics.

The majority in the media regard the members of the present administration as being less educated than them. They see it as an anti-intellectual government. For this reason, to a large degree, they think they have power over the politicians.

Honestly, Japan has no one to fall back on. No matter who succeeds Mr. Abe, there will be chaos, and he or she will not last long. However, it is also increasingly possible that the longer Mr. Abe continues to remain in office, the more Japan will become like China. This must be stopped.

He created the impression that he was doing something. He was able to pretend that way with his diplomacy. But the coronavirus put a stop to that and he has run out of options for his economic policies once called "Abenomics." He had his hopes on travel, tourism, and casinos, but the three C's proposed by epidemiologists (Closed spaces,

Crowded places, Close-contact settings) have squashed those too.

His basic thinking on how to realize economic prosperity is by getting people to shop more and spend more money in the leisure industry. But this thinking will collapse. The chaos will ensue. The economic collapse that will happen this year will be very severe. Depending on the company, some will really lose 99 percent of their revenue. And, while I cannot speak uniformly for all sectors, some parts of retail will see revenue increase and some in the IT fields will make money, but overall, there will be close to a 30 percent depression across the board in Japan and the U.S. too. It is said that Europe will see a 40 percent depression, so the trend worldwide will be toward contraction.

Therefore, it will be quite difficult for him to continue to run the country in this situation. Even if the present opposition parties form a coalition to do it, they will lose the people's confidence in no time. The opposition parties are a collection of people who have even less of a clue of how to revitalize the economy.

Japan's postwar politics will crumble and a great amount of deadwood will be cut

A

That leads me to the next question. Japan tends to try to overcome every economic problem by applying Keynesian economics, especially in the form of cash handouts.

YAIDRON

Yes, that's true.

A

It seems the majority of the world will also try to overcome this situation with Keynesian economics by giving out money. As the recession worsens and the world begins to feel that there are no solutions other than Keynesian economics, what prescriptions will we need?

YAIDRON

Keynesian economics has been regarded as the miraculous pill or a surgical operation that will rapidly revive an economy, just as Hitler resuscitated Germany's economy from its recession after World War I. However, just as it is gradually becoming apparent through the spiritual messages you put out, people will begin to see that it is actually similar to bad policies such as those of the first Qin Emperor.

The truth is, the essence of economy lies in freedom and equal opportunity. That is why there cannot be economic prosperity where there is no freedom or equality of opportunity. By freedom and equal opportunity, I mean the freedom for each citizen to start something as a small innovator or entrepreneur.

So, what the government does... A big government will be like a gigantic convoy trying to make sure there is not a single boat left behind, but this approach will not work for long. If it is a single airline company, then yes, it is possible for the government to save it. But saving every industry is impossible for any government.

Right now, the Japanese government has built up a bureaucratic system like the Edo shogunate, the old feudal military government. I believe this should be reset.

Bureaucracy has a habit of developing no matter what you do, but the effort must be made to keep it to a minimum. Bureaucracy actually destroys democracy, and in communism, it is a problem that crops up often. Politics dominated by bureaucracy tends to be autocratic. I believe this aspect will burst forth soon.

So, there will be the collapse of the mass media, the collapse of bureaucracy, and through them the collapse of Japan's postwar politics. The chaos will be quite unbearable to see. Major newspapers and major broadcasting companies will go under. Administration offices will lose the trust of the people and close. Many politicians who depended on the bureaucrats will find themselves having to come up with their own words, which means they can no longer carry out politics. A great amount of deadwood will be cut.

It might take 10 or even 20 years for all the deadwood to be cut. Japan too will see the beginning of an era of great chaos.

A religion with political and economic principles will rebuild the era

B

You spoke about how guaranteeing freedom and equal opportunity is important in economy. Outside of Japan, while these are lacking in China too, one would have to say that for example, Iran does not have these either, and it is the same in Saudi Arabia or Thailand, which are monarchies.

However, in Thailand, I hear that criticism is coming out little by little of not only the government but also of the royal family. Do you have plans for bringing economic prosperity through freedom and equal opportunity on a global scale? I would appreciate it if you could tell us about this.

YAIDRON

What I have told you is that, if the situation continues as it has this year, the world economy itself will experience a slow-down by anywhere from 30 to 40 percent. When the whole economy begins to shrink like a black hole, those places that are simply giving out money, places where social welfare has the entire country in a cradle and producing many idle citizens, and places where a form of autocracy such as a monarchy is practiced will all begin to feel the pressure of collapse.

There will be much chaos, but it is something you must go through. It cannot be helped. Only then will people begin to search for what they should rebuild the society upon.

Even if a hot nuclear war does not occur, there will occur many things such as a collapse brought about by an economic war, by a war of hegemony through knowledge, or by those who don't believe in God. Chaos will take over this planet. How to guide the world through it will be the next issue, and this issue also belongs to you.

A large part of it will depend on whether you can present a way of thinking about how a religion with faith in God and also with political and economic principles will help restructure the collapsing nations that are based on old religions or do not believe in God.

But the means is there. The ideas have already been presented. How humanity is able to turn those ideas into something real and tangible will determine the beginning of an age of rebuilding.

The Golden Age will be an age of destruction and new construction

YAIDRON
The Golden Age, therefore, is not a time when only good things happen for nothing. It is an age when alongside destruction and loss, the construction of something new will begin.

There will be things you have taken for granted that you will no longer be able to take for granted. For example, prior to Japan's defeat in WWII, praising the emperor was the norm, but that collapsed when Japan lost the war. After that, textiles, iron and steel, automobiles, and numerous other things spread widely. Repeatedly, many industries prospered and then declined. Similarly, what appears to be at its pinnacle now, you will see crumble before you.

The IT industry and the gaming industry look like they are turning a lot of profit, but they might be the next to go. You must start thinking about what the new thing should be after they collapse. Someone like Mr. Trump would probably say, "Go to church instead of watching fake news on Sundays." He would say you're better off praying at a church. In any case, this industry will see massive changes.

I think it's safe to assume that most everything that is massively popular at this time will head toward collapse, and during this process, people of new thought such as religious leaders or philosophers will appear and lead the people.

Scientism will soon collapse

A

You mentioned earlier that those with knowledge will have the highest power. When we look at the current state of Japan, intellectuals have degenerated or fallen back. Looking across the world, the number of true intellectuals has diminished too.

My question is about the knowledge gap. Aside from someone with a great quantity of knowledge, how can someone of high-quality knowledge fight back against this society? I would especially like to ask how to prevail against this view with Buddha's Truth, the knowledge that possesses the quality of Truth, and wisdom.

YAIDRON
As is shown in how there are fewer Japanese students choosing to study abroad in the United States today, it is a fact that in the area of knowledge, the added value attained by studying in the United States is declining.

Also related is the fact that America's philosophy is pragmatism. Often, Japanese students who go there study matters of practical reality that can produce practical gain. But when that is all that you learn, after returning to Japan, you most likely become a part of the materialists.

Regarding scientism, or perhaps many people view medical science in a similar way, even taking one example such as the coronavirus, a lot of the faith in medical science has crumbled. I think, however, there are still many who think that technological science remains omnipotent and stands above all knowledge and academic subjects. But when they face natural disasters on a global scale and intervention from outer space, they will come to see that this too was just like a castle built on sand.

Expect any "belief" in things that mere human beings have created, that is not a belief in God, to collapse. The things that everyone thought were most sure and certain will disintegrate, and those that have reached their pinnacle will also give way. I suggest that you perceive everything with that in mind.

Many space rockets made in the U.S., made in China, made in India, made in Russia, or elsewhere are being launched and used to check on their neighbors, but to us, those rockets are like a child's paper plane. It is a much undeveloped technology that takes nothing for us to do whatever we wish. Something to make you realize that may happen soon.

The future of science lies in religion

A

I believe our current scientific knowledge will lead us to an AI society. Will this share the same fate?

YAIDRON

When seen from our world, AI is, how should I say it, no different from *sugoroku* (a Japanese board game). It might appear to you as something incredibly advanced, but we have passed that stage far, far, far in the past.

For example, on this spacecraft we are on right now, there isn't a single computer. We no longer use such outdated things [*laughs*]. This spacecraft does not operate on a system like that. It is not easy to explain to you, but we fly through outer space by the power of our own spiritual energy, and a device that senses and responds to it.

This is something that today's AI cannot build. That is why you must surpass it. A human being's spiritual energy is actually much higher. You must create a device that senses and responds to it. The future of science does not lie in the science of today, but in religion.

It lies at the extension of what you call enlightenment or dharma power. That is where space science really lies.

7
The Single Ray of Light in the Age of Chaos

Human beings need to discover the mind and the soul

C

We are now close to the end of this interview. This is the last question from me.

You have taught us today that whatever is trending or popular now will collapse, and a decade or two of chaos will begin. You then said that, as a basic rule, we, humans, the ones living on Earth, must be the ones to decide the way forward out of our own free will. Could you give us guidelines for how to live through this chaotic era?

YAIDRON

First, humanity as a whole must discover the mind. They are hopeless unless they understand that at the center of themselves is the mind and discover the existence of the mind. Furthermore, the discovery of the mind must lead to the discovery of the soul. How much potential does the soul possess? Most Earthlings probably don't understand it any more than as a ghost of another world, but the soul possesses within it a far greater potential.

The soul can travel through the Spirit World by itself. It can make itself appear in this world. It can travel in an instant through the multidimensional space of this universe. Such is the soul. It possesses many wondrous functions. Unless you uncover this, you will remain forever far from stepping into the society based on future science.

Also, while I was not able to elaborate enough on the last topic, there is another world aside from the world you are living in, called the flip-side universe. I believe you are not aware enough about this yet, but there are those who are adding to and taking advantage of the chaos here on Earth from the flip-side universe. We are fighting against them too.

You must know there are all kinds of battles and races happening in the world invisible to you, yet you are completely oblivious to it. You are just like the people in the past who believed that they are living in a geocentric world, thinking that the world is flat like a table and around it, the stars, sun, and moon revolve. You are thinking in a similar way.

You think what you can see and touch is all there is, and all your thoughts and actions are within that scope. But you are now entering the age when you must take a leap. The one who shows you the doorway to such a world is the Savior of today. This you must know.

It may feel sad to see what is thriving now and the things everyone believes are certain and true crumble away. But at the same time, it will signify the birth, creation, and formation of something new. A new genesis will begin. Know this, and be ready for this.

The mission of disciples is to spread to every corner of the world the Savior's descent and His teachings

YAIDRON

We can do anything, you know. Floods, earthquakes, tsunamis, volcanic eruptions, and meteor strikes. All things are possible. If we wanted to reduce the human population, we can bring back dinosaurs too. Anything is possible. All we have to do is make them appear.

If we unleashed a lot of dinosaur-like creatures on the surface of the Earth, a lot of people and animals will be eaten. We can really make anything happen. You will be made to know that you are like animals in a zoo.

In order to snip the source of your arrogance, you will come to experience some setbacks, failures, and confusion. To be a ray of light in the midst of such times is precisely the mission of Happy Science. So, I tell you this: spread that light to the end of the world.

Tell people, "The light still exists. It is here. The light is shining, here and now. The Age of the Sun is still continuing." Teach them that. That is important. To the end of the world and to every country, spread the fact that the Savior is here and share His teachings. That is the mission of disciples.

You will never be able to fulfill your mission if you work like you are in a company with the economic principles of just running your organization. Such a way of working can exist as a given and as a suborganization, but your true mission is to teach to the whole world, to the nearly 200 countries of the world, that the Savior is here, to teach them the outline of His teachings, and to show them the direction humanity should head in into the future.

What does the Savior deem as true and as false? Teach them how He judges what is true from false, right from wrong. That is what is needed.

Everything on Earth is a civilization experiment happening on a single planet embraced in a great cosmic love

A

Today's theme was, "With Savior." We have been taught that the descent of the Savior this time is not the usual, 3,000-year cycle, but the first in 150 million years. I understand that the Savior is here now as a result of a great and detailed Savior's plan. We would greatly appreciate it if there is anything you can reveal to us in regards to where we are now according to this great plan and what the future holds.

YAIDRON

Your sense of time and our sense of time are very different. I don't believe we stand on the same playing field. I am treated as a space being from another planet, but I do not live the same time as you do. I have flown here to the Earth's past, I was here when the world needed to be saved, chose such times and appeared in various eras to watch. I appear in the future too and watch. I am such an existence.

Therefore, the concept of time Earthlings have does not apply to us. In the time of Jesus Christ, in the time of Shakyamuni Buddha, in times before that, and in times of civilizations before this 10,000-year one, we have given our guidance in various forms. Even now, we can go back into the past, or go into the future.

I would like you to know that everything on Earth is a civilization experiment happening on a single planet in the galaxy, embraced in a great, great, cosmic love.

The current Savior on Earth is guiding even the Messiahs in other galaxies

YAIDRON

We transcend time and appear in various places and give our influence. But while the Savior of this Earth has certain limits while He is in a physical body, when He departs from it, when He takes a spiritual form and becomes a space being, He also works to teach the other Messiah-certified beings in other galaxies. You should know this. We are existences that influence each other mutually.

There are times when we come down to this world in a physical body, but it is only occasional and the purpose is to gain a sense of what it is like to be human. The real world is not like that.

So, know that the Messiah of the Earth is actually someone who also guides on other planets and in other galaxies as well. How far will the last teachings He gives go? That is what we are watching now.

When you look from a greater perspective, you will see that you do not need to worry about the future. Both the past and the future are, frankly, various simulations, and things are redone many times in many places. What happened in a civilization in the past on Earth is something that is happening now on a planet somewhere in the universe. And something that is happening now on another planet is something that is to come in the near future on Earth.

Our present job is to accumulate the results of all these civilization experiments on a cosmic level and turn them into the Wisdom of the Universe, so we are recording, preserving, and studying them. In this way, we are aiming for the evolution of all souls in the universe.

A
OK. Thank you very much for today.

YAIDRON
Yes.

8

My Remaining Job Is to Reveal the Secrets of the Great Universe

RYUHO OKAWA

[*Claps once.*] Thank you very much, Mr. Yaidron [*claps once*].

As expected, there were some differences. His awareness is on a different level from that of the souls of Earthlings.

We are sorry to have had to ask for assistance from a being of such a level to remove *ikiryo* of people in our organization quite often, and have asked him to help us with all other minor happenings too. But these are experiments on various things, I guess.

However, it is not easy to teach people about the existence of cosmic-level beings. It is difficult to teach people how such beings are real, not fiction. What I can say is that things will appear according to the level of our growth. If we remain at the current level, space beings will not be able to show themselves and walk together with Earthlings, side by side. So, I want to raise the level of awareness of Earthlings as a whole.

Even so, they appeared quite early on in our movement. They were mentioned from around the time *The Laws of the Sun* was first published and they are a part of the teachings of Happy Science that cannot be removed. I must also reveal the secrets of the Great Universe. I think this will be my remaining job.

We must make Earth a better experiment ground, but also, its future is open to various possibilities.

Mr. Yaidon also mentioned today that even though it is said in Japan that there is a conflict between academics and religion, and also science and religion, that's not how it should be. I want to use a drill to dig through it and somehow break through.

That's all [*claps once*].

A

Thank you very much.

ENDNOTE

1 Yaidron carries out the role of patrolling the author 24 hours a day, seven days a week. He repels evil spirits and devils that interfere with the author's work, and guards him during his missionary tours in Japan as well as overseas. The number of recorded spiritual messages and UFO readings of him has reached over 25 times. See Part II Chapter Three of *Spiritual Reading of Novel Coronavirus Infection Originated in China* (Tokyo: HS Press, 2020).

CHAPTER TWO

Earthlings Viewed from the Universe

Spiritual Messages from Yaidron

Originally recorded in Japanese on August 24, 2020, in the Special Lecture Hall of Happy Science in Japan, and later translated into English.

The situation when this chapter was recorded

A day after "With Savior" (Chapter One) was recorded on August 23, 2020, Yaidron visited Master Ryuho Okawa and gave another spiritual message to supplement the messages given on the previous day.

1
Asking Yaidron about His Work and True Form

On the spiritual message from Yaidron recorded on the previous day

YAIDRON

Usually, when you get a chance to interview space people, wouldn't you question them about how they look or what their life is like on their home planet?

A

I think all the interviewers were unsure if we could ask you about that.

YAIDRON

The questions you were asking me were not very different from what's usually asked to someone like Trump's guardian spirit. I understand that you need to publish the book urgently, but it was insufficient.

A

So, would it be acceptable to ask you questions like, "How tall are you in meters?"

YAIDRON

You have released many videos of UFOs coming from space, but you haven't yet asked me anything about the sorts of things that average humans want to know about space people and UFOs in those videos.

B

We have released a lot of information about you already in previous recordings.

A

But the information hasn't been conveyed in an organized, coherent form to the general public.

B

So, people who hear or read your messages for the first time cannot understand it, right?

A

Are you saying that we could ask more about you?

YAIDRON

I mean, I think the interviewers were incompetent.

On Planet Elder, your spiritual level determines your occupation

A

So, may we ask you some questions now? [*About 10 seconds of silence.*]

You have told us that you come from Planet Elder. What is your occupation on that planet?

YAIDRON

I'm like a top-grade judge and politician who judges right from wrong.

A

So, do you mean that politics are conducted even on Planet Elder?

YAIDRON

Yes.

A

Is it different from the current democracy (on Earth)? What sort of politics is conducted on your planet?

YAIDRON

Well, I could say that occupations differ according to one's spiritual level.

A

Occupations differ according to the spiritual level.

YAIDRON

Right.

A

So, then, does everyone know their own spiritual level?

YAIDRON

In a sense, democracy is based on the assumption that "everyone is blind." It's "voting done by blind people." Voters don't know what kind of people the candidates are. They elect people without being able to see anything other than what can be seen in this world. People are not aware of the nature of each candidate's soul when they vote. This is the difference.

A

Metatron[1] said that, on his planet, people do not lose their memories of the time before they were born. He said that people are born with a certain amount of awareness of the kind of soul they are and whether or not they are an angel. Is Planet Elder similar to that?

YAIDRON

On Earth, even people possessed by devils can become top politicians, bureaucrats, military officers, police officers, university professors, television presenters, and business executives. But on our planet, people are aware of each other's spiritual level, so they are selected for jobs based on it.

I mean, one's occupation is not decided at birth. We look at people's inherent potential and the spiritual status and condition that they have acquired through their training and work up until that point. And after this information is known to everyone, occupations and jobs are assigned based on it.

On Earth right now, people vote for and give power to politicians, but they do this without even knowing whether they are good or evil. The situation is exactly what Jesus Christ would call "the blind leading the blind." This is not the type of democracy we have in our world.

A

Then, does everyone know the states of others' minds to some extent?

YAIDRON

Yes, we do.

A

Yesterday, I remember you told us that the power of enlightenment or thought is what makes UFOs fly. Does that mean that such things are common and everyone is spiritual?

YAIDRON

Happy Science has revealed the structure of dimensions and various people's past-life, but is struggling to reflect them in this world.

A

On top of that, what matters is the state of a person's mind in this life.

YAIDRON

We have the ability to do "spiritual scanning."

A

Spiritual scanning?

YAIDRON

Yes. It is probably similar to your X-rays and CT scans. Once people are scanned, it is possible to see everything about them. For example, which spiritual realms they are from, the current state of their mind, all their spiritual possessions up until now, and how well they performed their jobs with the support of high spirits.

People on Earth have diversity but do not distinguish between high and low

B

On Earth, we completely forget everything when we are born, from our memories before birth and where our soul is originally from. Does that seem somewhat primitive to you?

YAIDRON

No, it is a type of civilization experiment, so I think that's one way. An experiment of democracy is being conducted to see whether or not you can find out what each other are like with the information concealed. The experiment is to see whether or not the masses make correct judgments. And if they are not correct, then the masses themselves will later suffer for it.

A

I see.

YAIDRON

Also, people sometimes make mistakes when judging whether or not those who hold power through the media are right or wrong. And when they make such a mistake, they will later suffer for it.

A
So those in the position to choose need the ability or are tested for their ability to judge others' character.

YAIDRON
Exactly. Also, take entertainers as an example. They excite tens of thousands of people, and their fans are willing to pay ¥10,000 (about $94) to see them in a concert. And while some singers may seem like angels, others are the exact opposite, like the "Painted Skin."[2] And it seems to me that people can't really tell the difference.

A
I agree. Right now, they don't have any way to make distinctions.

YAIDRON
People talk about diversity, and while the people on Earth definitely have diversity, people have no sense of

high and low. They can't tell the difference. A major reason for this is the severe decline in religious values right now. And in regard to politics, even though Happy Science is telling people which person is angelic and which is demonic, they can't tell the difference. In fact, in most cases, anything involving religion is seen as a negative.

This means that, if the separation of religion and state were the proper system, then the media would not report any political activities involving religion unless they think it is a criminal case. In other words, there has not been ordinary, unbiased reporting. It is obviously wrong to judge that all religions are bad, but no one is trying to verify this academically.

Yaidron's true form

A

Excuse me. When you came to us for the first time, I remember that you said you were a reptilian. Many people in Happy Science cannot believe that a reptilian who has made advancements in science and technology also has such a high level of enlightenment. I guess so. Do you have anything you would like to say about that?

YAIDRON

Well, we change our physical appearance in accordance to our job. It's not fixed.

A

So, in other words, people from Vega are not the only ones who can transform?

YAIDRON

It would be impossible to travel from far off in the universe with a physical body as you have on Earth.

A

Is that because you pass through the Spirit World?

YAIDRON

We have spiritual bodies that can change into physical form. That's also why we are able to give spiritual messages. We have spiritual yet physical bodies. We have physical yet spiritual bodies.

A
I believe that there is still a lot of contempt within Happy Science toward reptilians, and I am sure that there are even some people who see you that way.

YAIDRON
It (his form of a reptilian) is a kind of battle mode we change into when something evil appears.

A
I see.

B
So, in other words, you're not constantly in a form of a reptile that eats humans?

YAIDRON
We do not necessarily reside within reptilian bodies. We take the form that we think you will prefer to see or the form that you feel is necessary. For example,

if you have recently become fond of ogres that strike with thunder, then we will gradually begin to look like ogres. Then, when we encounter someone else, we change into a form that matches their preference.

B
Do you have horns? When we asked you before...

A
You said that you have two horns.

YAIDRON
Well... If I tell you, then you'll start focusing on horns next and become lost again.

A
Yes, you're right.

My current job is related to justice and judgment

A

But that was our first impression of you. So, we were wondering what kind of person you really are.

YAIDRON

Well, my job right now is related to justice and judgment. My current job is to determine what justice and judgment mean on Earth.

A

The fact that you have been providing so much protection for El Cantare shows that you have a relationship with Him, but how should we understand the relationship between you and El Cantare?

YAIDRON

Hmm. He once taught me on a training planet for Messiah.

A

And that planet was...

YAIDRON
You've never heard of it.

A
It's a planet that hasn't been mentioned yet?

YAIDRON
Unless you have powers that go further beyond this physical time and space, I don't think you would understand even if I told you.

B
Is the planet unrelated to R. A. Goal's[3] planet (Planet Andalucia Beta in Ursa Minor), which is also called "a training planet for Messiah"?

YAIDRON
You still only think in terms of planets, so there's not much I can do. How we see the universe is different from yours. When you look up at the night sky, all you see are scattered, twinkling stars. That's one way to look at the world, but the world that we see is different.

A
How does it look to you?

YAIDRON
For us, there is a different world unfolding.

C
To put it in terms of Happy Science teachings, should we understand that it is at the level of the galactic consciousness or the universal consciousness? So how you recognize the world is fundamentally different from ours?

YAIDRON
Hmm. Those forms of expression themselves are primitive.

C
So I guess that too is human-like.

A
Will the day ever come when Earthlings reach the level of space people?

YAIDRON

Well, as long as you think that going into space means boarding a rocket with your physical body, then you are not in the same world that we are in.

2

How Aware Are Earthlings from the Perspective of Space?

How would Yaidron describe the difficulty of conversing with Earthlings?

A

Yesterday, Master Okawa was very fatigued after recording your spiritual message. Is that because there is such a wide gap between you and Earthlings?

YAIDRON

Well, that's...

A

Do you mean we haven't been able to comprehend what you say?

YAIDRON

Well, communicating with you entails the same kind of difficulty that Columbus experienced when he landed on the West Indies and tried to converse with the locals.

C

So there's just too big of a difference?

YAIDRON

It's hard. It's really hard.

A

It's hard even for those of us listening. Would you say it's a bit similar to the descent to Earth of Japanese Shinto gods (as taught in Japanese Shintoism)?

YAIDRON

No, that's unrelated.

A

Oh, it's not. I see.

YAIDRON

They were somewhat lower-level entities. To descend with a physical body means that they are a little lower level.

B

You've previously mentioned that you can have showers in an instant on spacecraft, but does this refer to when you are in a physical form?

YAIDRON

[*Sighs.*] This is really tiring.

B

I'm sorry. You sometimes speak very specifically. But is that just out of expediency?

A

So far, you have been speaking in a way that Earthlings can understand, but are you... starting to get fed up remaining at this level the whole time?

YAIDRON

Well, to me, the kind of justice that you are asking about just sounds as if you are asking, "Can we cut off a lizard's tail because it will just grow back anyway?"

A

"Can we cut off a lizard's tail, because it will grow back anyway?"

YAIDRON

"Therefore, doesn't it constitute bodily harm?" That is how it sounds to us.

A

So, are you saying that we are weak?

YAIDRON

[*Sighs.*]

C

Or do you mean that we talk about trifle matters?

YAIDRON

You won't understand unless you compare it to something you are familiar with.

A

Oh, so you mean we can't comprehend the concept?

YAIDRON
Hmm.

Earthlings and space people have completely different understandings of physical and spiritual bodies

YAIDRON
[*About five seconds of silence.*] You really need to watch *10,000 BC* on U-NEXT (Japanese video distribution service). Because that's what you are like.

A
[*Laughs.*] I hear that the movie depicts the world of primitive people.

YAIDRON
We have no choice but to become mammoths to express ourselves.

B
But you haven't yet spoken with anyone other than interviewer A before. We tried to record a spiritual

message from you in front of an audience once, but you were displeased with the interviewers. So I guess it cannot be done with ordinary interviewers.

A

No, I can't do it, either. I guess it means that our points of view are really different. We are occasionally scolded by high spirits in the heavenly world as well. But it seems that this difference in understanding is even greater than that.

YAIDRON

In your understanding, spirits are entities that have come out of physical bodies, right?

A

Yes.

YAIDRON

And this entity can dwell within a physical body when it's reborn from time to time, right?

A

Yes.

YAIDRON

Our understanding is different.

A

Your spirit is your true self, right?

YAIDRON

Unless you overcome the dichotomy in that way of thinking, you will never be able to travel from a star that is located hundreds of, or millions of light-years away like we can.

A

Once, I asked Lord Alpha, "Are you referring to physical or spiritual bodies?" and he said something like, "Both of them, of course." We didn't understand what he meant, but is this similar to what you are talking about?

YAIDRON

Well, Alpha... He's fine, but he's sort of like, *honyaku konnyaku*,[4] that you like.

A

Honyaku konnyaku?

YAIDRON

Yes. Alpha is like *honyaku konnyaku*.

A

What do you mean by that?

YAIDRON

He put it so that you can understand...

A

And expressed in such a way.

YAIDRON

Right. He just spoke as the Creator.

B

In Earth's history, there was a time when the Spirit World and this world were mixed together, right?

A

Yes, when they were merged together.

The reason people that split away from Planet Elder are on Earth

A

Going back to the political (electoral) system in Planet Elder, did your system evolve from the system like the one we have on Earth? Or did God create a completely different system from scratch?

YAIDRON

Well... I think you should hurry up and watch the movie *10,000 BC*.

B

If I remember correctly, a clear divide between this world and the other world was made after Lucifer fell to hell on Earth...

YAIDRON

That's not actually the case.

B

It's not? It might have been a means of expediency?

A

Did the people on Planet Elder not go through the process of evolution and have they always been the way they are now? Have they always been able to see through with that sort of spiritual eye?

YAIDRON

Well, it's very similar to the beginning of the movie *Superman*. Some of them split away from the planet when they became unable to live there. And opinions sometimes differ as well.

A

I see.

YAIDRON

We also sometimes send away or banish to other planets those who don't get along with us.

A
For example, people with what sort of values?

YAIDRON
[*Sighs.*] Please hurry up and watch *10,000 BC.*

A
But if you were in conflict, it means there were value differences, right?

YAIDRON
Yes... [*Exhales.*]

B
We have heard that a long time ago, (the soul of) En no Ozunu[5] came to Earth after being banished from Planet Elder.

A
We were told that "En no Ozunu was sent to Earth."

YAIDRON
Well, I think that is beyond En no Ozunu's ability to understand.

A
Ah, so En no Ozunu doesn't know why he was banished?

YAIDRON
He was only here about a mere 1,200 years ago. [*About five seconds of silence.*] He has no connection as to what had happened further back in time. He probably doesn't even remember anything.

A
But according to Master Okawa's teachings, a system was created for the Earth in which people forget their past when reincarnating. Does it mean that the systems for the training grounds of Planet Elder and Earth are different?

YAIDRON

[*Exhales.*] Our world is much farther in the future than yours. We are in the world of the future, and once we progress a little farther, we will enter a world in which there is no more evolution. In that case, some people will want to return to primitive times.

A

Is that why the Earth is necessary as a training ground for souls?

YAIDRON

Yes.

A

So the only people who come here are the ones that want to return to primitive times?

YAIDRON

They are people who want to do it all over again. Yes.

A

Then what about the people who do not want to do it all over again?

YAIDRON

They haven't come.

A

Ah, so they are watching from above (from UFOs)?

YAIDRON

They are not born as Earthlings.

A

But their own planet will be destroyed, right?

YAIDRON

On the other hand, though, they observe and record the various civilization experiments taking place here and there.

A

So, they are like those who fly around in UFOs, right?

YAIDRON

Some of them, yes.

A

I've heard that, a long time ago, a force came from Andromeda to battle, and Planet Zeta, the home of the Reptilians in the Magellanic Clouds, was destroyed, but Planet Elder successfully defended itself.

YAIDRON

Yes, but the details of that would be difficult to explain. That will sound like the world of science fiction to you, so I don't really want to talk about it.

A

I see.

The pitifulness of Earthlings who consider devotion to machines to be human progress

YAIDRON

[*Exhales.*] You're really behind... The Earth is really behind.

A
After yesterday's spiritual message, you felt the extent of how far behind Earthlings are... Looking at the current situation with the coronavirus, people on Earth are trying to continue to live by coexisting "with the coronavirus," without awakening to what they really should. I'm sure it must be deeply tiring for you to see humanity trying to get through this while the evil of China remains concealed.

YAIDRON
Well, that's...

A
Are we even farther behind than you expected?

YAIDRON
Hmm... [*Sighs.*] Well, at this rate, even the efforts of Ryuho Okawa will be in vain. Well... This type of evolution—Earth's evolution—is difficult.

A
And even though people need to become a little more

spiritual and start to call the name of God during this coronavirus crisis, they seem to be going in the exact opposite direction overall.

YAIDRON
[*Sighs.*]

A
Do you feel that the Earthlings are in great danger?

YAIDRON
The Earthlings are at a level where they can't tell whether Xi Jinping's actions are the same as those of ancient barbarians or not.

A
Right. As you said yesterday, the more intellectual a person is, the less they are able to perceive the truth.

YAIDRON
They are stupid.

A

And they see President Trump as the stupid one.

C

First of all, it's stupid to think that the Earth is progressing. It's headed for destruction...

A

Right. It means people are trying to make progress in the exact opposite direction.

YAIDRON

People think that progress means entering the world of materialism, atheism, agnosticism, science, and technology. They think that "devotion to machines" means human progress, which makes me pity them. They had experienced similar civilizations already before coming to the Earth, but I just feel surprised at the level they are still at even when they have been here for so long.

A

Are there any other planets that are this far behind?

YAIDRON
I'm sure there are.

A
Oh, there are?

YAIDRON
There are some planets where only primitive lifeforms exist. But seeing the entire Earth, how do I say it... being this threatened by something as insignificant as a bat-borne virus is a little hard for us to believe.

The difficulty of teaching people who are incapable of understanding

A
I think that you, R. A. Goal, and Metatron all have a deep understanding between right and wrong. Do you mean that this sense of value is related to enlightenment?

YAIDRON

Yes. Enlightenment includes science. Because it's about learning the Truth. It's also about learning what Truth is.

A

You're saying that, once we learn the Truth, learn about the existence of the Creator and learn that we have been created, that's when we will begin to gain insight to see what is wrong and what is right.

YAIDRON

A while ago, you were watching the UFO video recently released by the U.S. The video showed a UFO entering an area off the coast of San Diego where U.S. aircraft carrier training was being conducted. You saw that it could move around so freely that there was nothing that could be done about it, right?

A

Yes. (Note: Interviewer A was watching a documentary TV series called "Unidentified: Inside America's UFO Investigation.")

YAIDRON

That's what UFOs are like. To put it bluntly, the jet fighters and other armaments you have on Earth seem like ants to us. That's how big of a difference there is. It's hard because—it's not just that the words are incomprehensible to you—the concepts themselves cannot be conveyed.

A

I see.

YAIDRON

But the U.S. military seems to at least understand that they are outclassed.

A

The people who witnessed that UFO reportedly said, "That mysterious object has no wings." So, from the point of view of us Earthlings, we wonder, "How can it even fly?"

YAIDRON

It has no wings.

A

It has no wings. It has no windows.

YAIDRON

It produces no heat.

A

Right, right.

YAIDRON

It has no windows. It can move in any direction. And when it accelerates, it covers a great distance in a second.

A

(Observing the movement of a UFO and estimating the distance,) It can move at 6,000 kilometers per hour.

YAIDRON

There is no way that humans could be in it. They wouldn't understand anything. It cannot be comprehended.

A

I get the impression that we wouldn't understand anything.

YAIDRON

None of it. All of it wouldn't make any sense.

Well… I do pity you. I sympathize with you for the fact that you are incapable of comprehending. I would appreciate it if you could somewhat get a sense of how difficult it is to preach teachings to people who are incapable of understanding them.

A

So, after giving a spiritual message yesterday, you were burdened with the same pain all night long too, didn't you?

C

We are very sorry about that. (C was also an interviewer during the previous day's spiritual message [Chapter One].)

A
We are sorry.

YAIDRON
Well, it is like you giving a sermon to a stag beetle.

A & C
[*Laughs.*]

B
Even Lord Heem[6] from Planet Vega, who descended before and gave a spiritual message in front of an audience, didn't feel like talking to the interviewers to begin with.

A
Yes, you're right.

B
He didn't answer our questions much.

YAIDRON
How sad. It is hard being a Savior on Earth. It's really hard.

A

What's more, there are even people who cannot understand Lord Heem (or think he is far behind). Even though, from his point of view, he is way out of reach from us.

YAIDRON

Oh well...

Feeling tired of Earth's primitiveness

A

How does El Cantare call you? Yaidron?

YAIDRON

Well, that's what I'm called right now. But actually, it's time for El Cantare to...

A

You mean, He's done enough?

YAIDRON

I'm not sure whether I should say, "He's done enough." What I mean is that I have started to feel sorry for El Cantare being placed on the Earth. It's a world with a lot of restrictions.

A

Yes, you're right.

YAIDRON

I feel sorry.

A

It seems like, no matter how hard El Cantare works, people just have no interest in listening to Him.

YAIDRON

It's not going well at all.

A more overbearing and oppressive person could employ the kinds of bullying tactics used on ancient people. For example, saying, "If you don't do what I say, then I am going to severely punish you." Even for us, we are losing motivation, so we can't really say anything.

To be honest, what you need is someone who acts like an ogre. You need an ogre with a club that will bop people on the head when they do something wrong.

A

Yes. When you consider the level of this world, people still need ogres to motivate themselves, just like in the Japanese folk tale. It seems like people are still at the level where they need to be told, "Bad things will happen if you are thinking only about yourself," and "Bad things will happen if you're greedy."

C

Right. People don't even stick to the moral of such a level most of the time.

YAIDRON

I can't tell whether they are evolving or degenerating. And they don't think about how to improve civilization by choosing a moral code by themselves. The other day, I came and intervened during a spiritual message that said, "I can do whatever I want as long as I chant 'Namu Amida Butsu,'" but it comes to show how primitive Earthlings are for such teachings to spread. I can't explain enough how primitive this is.

A
Ah...

YAIDRON
Ah, there really is primitiveness. It's extreme. It is very tiring. It truly is.

3
Planet Elder and the Flip-Side Universe

On Planet Elder, the coronavirus would be disinfected in one second

A
This is completely off-topic, but you are from Planet Elder, right?

YAIDRON
I'll leave it like that.

A
But you have a much longer history, right?

YAIDRON
I can't show you a sketch of the universe. You wouldn't be able to understand it at all. I mean, it's unbelievable that you are being killed by a virus, which doesn't even have a soul.

A

If a virus like the coronavirus broke out on Planet Elder, how would everyone act?

YAIDRON

It would be over in one second.

A

How so?

YAIDRON

Through disinfection.

A

On hearing that, an ordinary Earthling would think, "Oh, of course. Their science is so advanced that they must have such medicines that kill viruses." But that is not what you mean, is it?

YAIDRON

First of all, the process of entering a humanoid space person, replicating itself, and killing the host by invading the lungs would not be possible. There is no way something like that could get inside.

A
You mean, everyone can distinguish between viruses and their own...?

YAIDRON
Viruses are inferior to living organisms.

A
So, they wouldn't even be able to enter your bodies?

YAIDRON
Basically, a viral infection is very similar to spiritual possession. It seems like humans are something like compost in which they are culturing earthworms. It's hard to believe.

B
So, you mean that viruses are inherently incapable of entering the bodies of people from Planet Elder?

C

Viruses don't grow in your bodies as they do with the Earthlings?

YAIDRON

The way that viruses proliferate inside human bodies before spreading on to more and more hosts is exactly like how people 100 years ago envisioned an invasion by space people. But it is suspicious whether viruses themselves even have souls.

At any rate, the very fact that viruses can spread like that is shocking to us.

A

Are you saying, "Can't Earthlings even detect viruses?"

YAIDRON

You get taken over and killed by such things.

B

So, do people from Planet Elder not catch things like influenza or a cold?

YAIDRON

It may be OK for there to be lower-level beings, but they can't invade higher-level ones.

A

Ah, you mean, you are on a completely different wavelength, so you are never possessed by viruses.

YAIDRON

Watching the daily news these days, it seems like humans are on the verge of becoming slaves to the virus. The virus is more powerful. It is as though the virus might become God.

A

You're definitely right about that.

YAIDRON

To us, it is so ridiculous that we are at a loss for words.

"We are the beginning of life" "We have never died" "We live forever"

A

So, you don't get cancer, either?

YAIDRON

[*Exhales deeply.*] There are cases where we must end our soul training in this world.

A

You said that, on Planet Elder, there isn't much difference between the physical and spiritual bodies.

B

Don't you get sick before you die?

YAIDRON

Well, we don't really understand what it means to die.

A

So, you just keep living as you are?

B

Do you ascend into a spiritual body, like ascending to a higher dimension?

YAIDRON

I have no set lifespan. It's infinite. I have more memory than you can trace. We live forever.

A

May I ask a question from the current perspective of an ordinary Earthling? If you live forever, then does that mean married people stay with their partner forever?

YAIDRON

[*Sighs.*]

A & B

[*Laugh.*]

A

I just thought, "Why should I even bother anymore?" I mean, it's what an ordinary Earthling would wonder.

YAIDRON
[*Sighs.*] We are the beginning of life.

A
The beginning of life?

YAIDRON
Yes. We have never died. Although we have taken different forms, we have never died. We live forever.

B
But according to your past messages, you have someone like a spouse, right?

YAIDRON
Well, as a matter of convenience, depending on the civilization.

A
Ah, I see. You live forever, but even on Planet Elder, civilizations come and go.

YAIDRON

Sometimes, we appear differently from civilization to civilization.

B

Then, does your spouse change too?

YAIDRON

Well... That's...

A

That is how we would think, based on our sense of things.

B

Do you have more than one spouse?

YAIDRON

The idea of a spouse is already...

A

Do you have any children?

YAIDRON

...a very low-grade topic, so...

A

Before, you said that you have a father and a mother.

YAIDRON

Ah... Yes, if necessary, it's possible.

A

Sorry.

YAIDRON

For example, we will do that if we cannot establish a relationship in any other way.

A

Ah, with people from other planets?

YAIDRON

Yes. We sometimes appear that way to people who wouldn't understand otherwise.

El Cantare recognizes the universe as a soap bubble

A

So, after all, were you created as a part of the light that split off from El Cantare?

YAIDRON

Hmm... According to El Cantare's recognition, this dark universe that you see is like a small soap bubble. The whole universe is like a single, tiny cell. But you are in a world where you can't comprehend what this single cell is a part of.

B

You once said that there is a female savior on Planet Elder named Maitrey.

YAIDRON

Hmm, well...

B

Was it just an expedient expression?

YAIDRON
Our advanced-level people become saviors when they go to other planets.

A
What is El Cantare called on Planet Elder?

YAIDRON
Huh?

A
In other words, the Creator. On Earth, He is called El Cantare.

YAIDRON
Right now, He is called "the One on Earth."

A
Ah, so they think that He has gone to Earth.

YAIDRON
Because He is bound to Earth right now. He is responsible for the entire Earth.

A
Has El Cantare been on Planet Elder?

YAIDRON
Yes, well... [*Sighs.*] He should graduate already.

A
From Earth?

YAIDRON
He should graduate this universe already.

From your point of view, we are unidentified entities that freely appear and disappear. But considering our true form, at the very least, when we reveal ourselves and speak, act, obtain food and hydrate ourselves as human-like organisms, it is similar to you being reborn into the earthly world with a physical body.

B
It probably means that it is not a matter of when El Cantare came to the Earth, but rather, that He exists on several planets simultaneously or is omnipresent throughout the universe.

A
I see.

YAIDRON
It is too much of a hassle (to explain). Maybe you should just tell everyone to pray, "Namu Amida Butsu."

A & B
[*Laugh.*]

The origin of the dark-side universe is the "Creator" of the dark part of humanity

A
There is also the dark-side universe, right?

YAIDRON
Yes.

A
Was the dark-side universe created at some point?

YAIDRON

Well, the universe is like a single cell, and there exist various such cells. There is an entity that is eroding those cells. These universe cells are bound together by the power of love, and there is an entity trying to destroy this bond.

A

Did God approve of and create that energy form which works to destroy it, although the word "create" may be inappropriate? Or, are you saying that such a function did not originally exist, but it appeared at some point?

YAIDRON

[*Sighs.*] You know, the dark parts of yourself in the day. There is "the Creator" behind them.

A

Ah, I see. So, it's the result of many people emitting those things.

YAIDRON

Throughout the day, people experience various emotions. They get angry, they scream, they rage, they get jealous, they go crazy from hunger, or sometimes they collapse out of fatigue. These feelings come from a source. That is the origin of the dark-side universe.

A

Was it created by those sorts of thoughts and feelings from Earthlings and other space people?

YAIDRON

It was created by neither Earthlings nor space people.

A

But didn't we create it?

YAIDRON

No. It has its own source, and this source is inside you all. That's all.

A

Are you saying there is dualism (of light and darkness)?

C

From what you just said, it sounds like there is an entity that created the evil part.

YAIDRON

Light only cannot make up the universe.

A

So, evil has its own Creator?

YAIDRON

[*Sighs.*] Where light and darkness collide, there appears a shockwave, and this shockwave gives birth to existences.

B

Then, are you saying that there are both light and dark parts in our souls?

YAIDRON

Yes.

A

It's like "Humanoid Monster Bem (a character in a Japanese anime)."

YAIDRON

Yes, it's similar to that.

A

That story is based on the idea that having both good and evil is what makes us human.

YAIDRON

Right.

A

Is that so?

YAIDRON

The two are always in a tug of war.

C

Then, when evil feelings grow within humans, they are at risk of getting their value system overturned.

YAIDRON

Right. And our job is to reverse that and restore balance.

4

Asking about Yaidron's Role and UFOs

About his connection to Moses and Yahweh

A

Excuse me. Sorry to ask you something so trivial, but when trying to understand you, some people see you as a reptilian that feeds on anima[7].

YAIDRON

You eat steak rice bowl when you get hungry too, don't you?

A

Yes. Humans also eat. Are you saying that it's the same type of thing?

YAIDRON

Well, if we do not absorb some element of this world, we won't be able to exist in this world.

A

Ah. So, when you are in your UFO up in the sky in this world, you take a worldly form for the time being.

YAIDRON

For the time being, yes.

A

Do you have any connection to Moses?

YAIDRON

I sometimes appeared during his time, too.

A

Ah. So, you're not actually connected to Moses himself?

YAIDRON

I'm like the pillar of fire that guided Moses.

A

I recall that, when you first came, you said that Yahweh also has a connection with that planet.

YAIDRON

I said so because that's the only way to explain it in a way that you'll understand. It's like expressing myself as "I'm like an *oni* (ogre) wielding a club and wearing a tiger-striped loincloth."

A

I recall you mentioning it during our first UFO reading with you, but do you have any connection to Yahweh?

YAIDRON

Yes. I am like the combination of a judge, prosecutor, and statesman. So, a part of my function overlaps with a part of Yahweh's. Anyway, I am your most favorite type of person. I destroy evil.

A

[*Laughs.*]

Yaidron creates and enforces rules of justice

B

You are a judge and statesman. Does that mean, even

on Planet Elder, there are people who do bad things? Or does it mean that you reconcile the differences in value systems?

YAIDRON
I create the rules of the era.

A
You create rules.

YAIDRON
Those who do not comply with them get driven out. It inevitably means they become evil.

B
I see.

YAIDRON
In other words, if we leave them on the planet, they will end up in prison. But if they leave, they will be exiled somewhere.

A

So, after all, you are one of the people who create those kinds of rules and determine what God's justice is, right?

YAIDRON

I also enforce the rules.

A

You also enforce them. I see.

YAIDRON

When we can let people go, we sometimes send them to a planet that matches their level, if it is available. It's immigration.

Some of the so-called reptilian kind were sent to Earth because their wavelength matched Earth's wavelength at the time.

C

Incidentally, you mentioned there are many people on Planet Elder who would be Messiah-level figures if they went to other planets. What other kinds of jobs or roles are there in terms of Earth's?

A

Good question. They can't all be judges, right?

YAIDRON

Some focus more on creative work. Some people have the role to maintain the current balance or a sense of stability. Others have the role to create new things, things that don't yet exist. Yet, some others embody something similar to the types of tasks that machines, robots, and computers currently perform in your world.

Jealousy from disciples who want to sit next to God

A

I don't want to classify you as average people on Planet Elder, so I'll treat you as (a particular energy body called) "Yaidron." When do you feel happiness or joy?

YAIDRON

[*Sighs.*] Actually, rarely. It's been unpleasant every day. So, I don't feel much happiness or joy. I'm always doing the dirty work.

A

That's true. Really, it...

YAIDRON

It's always, always like that. Recently, it feels like I'm being made to compete with the red oni of Kusatsu.[8]

A

No, we are not making you compete. The level of enlightenment that we Earthlings have is low, so unfortunately, we are having you do such work.

YAIDRON

[*Sighs.*] There is no other work I can do, so it can't be helped.

A

Yesterday, you mentioned the phrase, "With Savior."

In your spiritual message before that, the title was, "The Attitude of Protecting the Lord." You always seem to use phrases like that. Are these your most-valued phrases?

B
Do you mean that you are happy when you are protecting El Cantare and when He makes progress in His work?

YAIDRON
[*Sighs.*] I must choose my words carefully, otherwise, there will be trouble. I mean, the people of Earth have the feeling of jealousy, and when it all comes together, it can be pretty powerful. It's quite hard to deal with.

A
You're right. Every time that we record you, including yesterday, I definitely get the feeling that some people are jealous of you. They are jealous, or rather, it's like they are competing against you. I get the feeling that they are saying, "Still, we are more important than you."

YAIDRON
That's why, as much as possible, I try to provide protection behind the scenes, in a round-about way, instead of taking a major role. In some aspects, many disciples get jealous of me. Many of them want to sit on the right or left of God. So, there's no room for me there.

A
Those might be key phrases for understanding you. Now, we cannot protect Master without the power of space people.

YAIDRON
That is something only you can understand and express. Most people are still on a level like believing in viruses that they have never seen.

A
I definitely get that impression.

YAIDRON
Please study about how primitive people feel. That will help you understand them.

The video you saw earlier said something like, "When the U.S. aircraft began to track them and fly around, the group of UFOs escaped." But it's not that we fled; we just seemed to have disappeared before they knew it because the jets were so slow [*laughs*].

A

[*Laughs.*] So, inside the UFO, you are thinking, "Huh? They're not following us."

YAIDRON

It's as if a turtle is running and chasing us.

A

Are you surprised by how slow they are?

YAIDRON

Yes. We are on a completely different level.

Asking about Yaidron's UFO, which had stopped vertically

A

But even though so many UFOs have been witnessed, many people still cannot believe this very fact. Most people may not be able to see ghosts, but there are many cases where multiple people have witnessed UFOs at the same time. Even so, people are still wondering whether or not UFOs exist.

YAIDRON

Videos can be fabricated. All you have to do is show a shiny white object flying, right? It can be fabricated.

Happy Science is now attempting to express the feelings of space people in the same way as spiritual messages, but I think it's quite difficult for people to get up to your level.

A

That's true. The other day, when we were taking pictures of UFOs,* we got a picture of what looked like the UFO fleet of your and Metatron's ships shining in a vertical position. What kind of UFOs were you in?

YAIDRON

UFOs fly when they are horizontal. They stop when they are vertical. They are in a vertical position, so that they will remain stationary.

A

I see. It was rare to see them vertical.

YAIDRON

They stopped to observe.

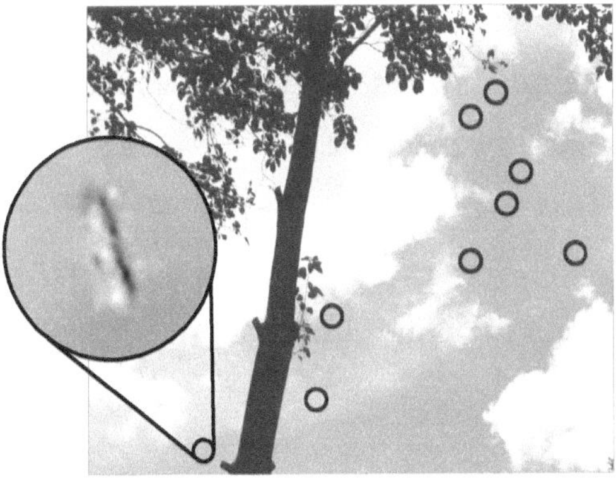

* A photo of UFOs captured by the author on August 10, 2020. A fleet of UFOs appeared. The circles indicate the position of the UFOs.

B

When they are vertical, they stop, and when they fly, they become horizontal. Is that right?

A

Is that why they turned vertical?

YAIDRON

When flying, they move horizontally. They can stop if they turn vertical.

A

Excuse me. This is in the sense of Earthlings again. When we were discussing this the other day, Master said, "These probably go back and forth between vertical and horizontal." And at that time, I wondered, "What happens to the people inside?"

YAIDRON

Nothing happens. It's the same either way.

A

Oh, nothing changes.

B

I guess the space inside the UFO is designed so that it does not change much.

YAIDRON

Right.

B

One video footage showed them being horizontal and then going vertical.

A

Were there other instances of that?

YAIDRON

We can be however we want. UFOs can also rotate. If they were a merry-go-round, we would get dizzy, you know?

A

So, you are stationary. In other words, the outer part rotates or changes position.

YAIDRON

Right. The outer part rotates, but we can be however we want. It's hard to explain. Our recognition is different from yours.

UFOs ascend to another dimension when they exceed the speed of light

A

Some space people said they get motion sickness when riding in a UFO. But people of your level do not get motion sickness, right?

YAIDRON

The ones who get motion sickness might be those who are riding as passengers. They don't have their own craft, so they are riding in other space people's.

A

I see.

YAIDRON
In the eyes of Earthlings, UFOs are not much different from ghosts. UFOs appear and disappear, right? Ghosts appear in this world and disappear, too. They're similar. Actually, in terms of space-time, UFOs sometimes go beyond the third dimension. They are still third-dimensional entities while they are flying at speeds up to 10 times the speed of a jet in the third dimension. But when they accelerate, they can surpass the speed of light. When they do, they slip out of the third dimension and ascend to another dimension.

A
OK.

The Chinese goddess Dongting Lake Niangniang is aware of space people

A
I'm going to completely change the subject again.

YAIDRON
Please don't ask me whether or not miso ramen tastes good.

A
[*Laughs.*] I think I remember asking you a lot about food before.

Recently, we frequently talk spiritually to Dongting Lake Niangniang.[9] She said she knows you. She said you occasionally come to replenish your water. Is that true from your standpoint, too?

YAIDRON
[*Sighs.*] Well, she is a being of another dimension.

A
Do you know her?

YAIDRON
She is much easier to talk to, compared to all of you.

A
I see. So, you know her, right?

YAIDRON
Even if you are a being of another dimension, if you are bound to this world like ghosts are, you would have a hard time recognizing us. But beings of higher dimensions are usually aware of us. So, when we happen to go there, we sometimes talk.

A
You do?

YAIDRON
It's possible.

A
I see. OK.

YAIDRON
It also depends on their level of recognition. If we come within their scope of recognition, we can converse. But someone like *Okiku* or *Oiwa*, who you see as the ghosts of the Edo period, will have difficulty in having a conversation with us even if we met. They won't know what we are.

Anyway, people would probably classify us as *yokai* (monsters) or something like that, too [*laughs*].

A
That's true [*laughs*]. If they saw you.

YAIDRON
They wouldn't understand. Japan has many stories about *kappa* (water imp), but those were most likely Greys.

A
Ah. So, Greys...

YAIDRON
Japanese people would definitely see Greys as kappa.

A
You're absolutely right. They both have short statures.

YAIDRON
The thing that looks like a turtle shell on their backs is probably a part of the device they use when

traveling through space. I think there are cases of people seeing that.

5

What Is the Earth in the Universe?

The conflict between China and other countries looks like nothing more than a fight between horned beetles

YAIDRON

Well, there have been beings that came to the Earth from different planets to become leaders, but were removed from their leadership positions and have instead continued to exist while adapting themselves into various forms and shapes.

However, the Earth is now beginning to get a little bit cramped. I'm starting to feel that something needs to be done [*sighs*].

C

Does it feel cramped because of how low Earthlings' level of state of mind is, seemingly being so primitive?

A
Is it because we are not rising in level?

YAIDRON
Well, you're just really tiresome.

C
I see.

YAIDRON
Even looking at the conflict between China and other countries, it just looks like nothing more than a fight or a wrestling match between horned beetles and stag beetles over a patch on a tree where sap seeps out. It seems like that.

Members of the Interplanetary Alliance are watching over the Earth from various standpoints

A
In the beginning, we heard that there exists an Interplanetary Alliance. Then, later, you, R. A. Goal,

and Metatron came and visited us. Are you all from the same framework as the Interplanetary Alliance?

YAIDRON

There is no need to teach Earthlings all the ins and outs of the Interplanetary Alliance, nor is there any need to tell you who the leaders are or what they are doing. It should be enough for you to know that beings that are visiting you are those who are of your interest.

A

Right, I see. I understand.

YAIDRON

I mean, there are beings watching over you every day like this, and others who are watching over people living on the islands of Palau, for example.

A

Yes. I understand.

YAIDRON

Sorry. You may have felt my vibration of fatigue.

C

No, we are sorry for putting a burden on you, continuing from yesterday.

A

After you came to give a message to Earthlings (through spiritual message), Master Okawa also said, “I’m sure that it was considerably fatiguing for Yaidron as well to talk while viewing the current state of the world.” And those who listen to you might wonder, “How can we understand this entity that is unlike the high spirits in heaven? Is it OK to just believe in him?”

YAIDRON

Even we sometimes experience something similar to despair and feel like flying off alone somewhere in the universe.

A

You mean after observing the Earth?

YAIDRON

I mean after getting involved with you.

A & C
[*Smile wryly.*]

YAIDRON
Too much, too much... How do I say? You're almost like elementary school first graders who can't perform addition or subtraction. Hmm... it's tough. I pray that Master Okawa doesn't feel as I do. When interacting with Happy Science staff members, I hope that he doesn't end up getting driven to enter the flip-side universe or fly off to the ends of the universe out of despair.

A
But that feeling... Well, yes, you're right.

Are Earthlings no different from the panda family at Ueno Zoo?

C
Despite how fatigued you feel at the state of Earth, you still every day...

A
That's right. We appreciate you coming today too.

C
Yes, we are very grateful that you've come.

B
Thank you very much.

C
Is that because we must truly value the fact that the Savior El Cantare is still working on Earth?

YAIDRON
[*Sighs.*] You all are truly no different from the panda family living at Ueno Zoo.

C
[*Laughs.*]

YAIDRON
That's how you are seen. Beings in the universe look at you and think, "Oh look at the Earth. They still get pregnant, give birth, and raise children."

B & C
[*Laugh.*]

A
That's true. I guess places that have further progressed probably don't follow that style. I'm sure it's a lot less work.

YAIDRON
Yes. There are other planets besides Earth, where their civilization experiments involve beings reincarnating and dwelling inside physical bodies without being able to see the other world. There are truly both places where only souls exist and places where souls go back and forth between the Spirit World and the material world.

A
However, when Master Okawa gave the lecture, "The Opening of the Space Age" (See *The Laws of Bronze* [New York: IRH Press, 2019]) in the summer of 2018, he said, "The Earth may not be so advanced, but in terms of spirituality, it has things that even beings from other planets can learn from."

YAIDRON

Well, you should be careful, though, because he was being a bit diplomatic.

A

It's more or less like, "Your level of spirituality is also low." Earthlings are materialistic now.

YAIDRON

If he at least doesn't put it like that, then...

B

Maybe he meant it in comparison with primitive reptilian type people.

C

Right.

A

I see. It was foolish of me to talk to you about our spirituality.

YAIDRON

From our point of view, we think El Cantare has worked so hard. He's accepted so many diverse beings.

A

I agree.

YAIDRON

He seems to do far beyond what would reasonably be expected because if he didn't like them, he could just tell them to stay away.

Experiments on soul creation and soul evolution that are conducted on Earth

A

When I learned about each planet (through UFO readings, etc.), I realized that there are many planets where similar species seem to gather together. But do you mean that the Earth is more like a melting pot for diverse people?

YAIDRON

Yes, I guess you can put it that way. If someone goes to a planet with only horned beetles and stag beetles, they would be an alien on that planet. I'm sure there are places like that. On a planet where plants and trees have only begun to grow, horned beetles and stag beetles which have appeared there would be the most highly evolved creatures.

A

Well, Master Okawa's love is truly deep.

YAIDRON

I think that soul creation is being conducted on Earth. I believe that an experiment on the process of soul evolution that takes several hundred million years is also being conducted on beings of various levels—from minuscule through to various advanced levels—that are brought into existence and instilled with souls.

Next, they are evolved to the level of a house pet, and then to a human being. I think this is the kind of experiment on soul evolution that is being conducted.

A
I see.

YAIDRON
But I think that, if too many exist, then—as has happened in the past—it could result in the destruction of civilization. You may be on the verge of that right now.

Moles will keep living even if the sunlight does not reach the surface of the Earth. They will survive. If this leads organisms that cannot survive without sunlight to go extinct, moles will then begin to evolve in their own way. They will create an underground empire, and eventually will start thinking about coming up to the surface. This is just speculation. There are any numbers of examples of these sorts of life experiments.

When it comes to UFOs, things are difficult, and your civilization cannot handle them. The only method available is for a small handful of people to act as interpreters and guides. Because you probably wouldn't want to see space people walking down the street however they want or stop walking at the crossing and so on.

A

[*Laughs.*] It would be quite a shock because they looked different from us.

Space people's technology is capable of creating and teleporting water

A

We are terribly sorry for taking so much of your time today. This is one of our closing questions, but there are people on the Earth who claim that, for organisms to exist elsewhere in space, there needs to be water there, but is it true that organisms cannot exist without water? Are other forms of space people like that as well?

YAIDRON

Actually, it is possible to make as much water as you want.

A

Oh! So, for a race that has the technology to create water, even if their planet doesn't have water, they're not worried because they can just make it themselves, right?

YAIDRON

Water can be made. With technology of our level, we are already capable of freely combining anything on the periodic table to make things. If we think about making something, we can.

A

I believe that some people even say, "Space people don't exist because there is no evidence of water on other planets."

YAIDRON

If we are going to give rise to life on a planet to allow it to live there, we create water.

A

Ah. So you can create it.

YAIDRON

We can, and we can also move it from planet to planet. If there is a planet that has water but is not needed as the site of a life experiment, it is possible to move that water to some other planet in an instant.

A

Wow. The fact that you teleport water is amazing.

YAIDRON

When we do, the new planet is suddenly struck with a flood, just like the story of Noah. Anything of that level is possible. Regrettably, though, saying that makes it sound like you're returning back to your primitive age. It pains me to say very much, so I can't express it.

The reason the Earth has become monitored and protected

A

We are truly grateful for your time yesterday and today.

YAIDRON

The Earth has the role of creating, growing, and diversifying life, and in that sense, it is a valuable life experiment site. So, space people come from all across space and think that they have to protect this cradle of life. And some are even born here.

That's why the Earth has become monitored and protected. So, if you destroy your civilization in a good meaning, then it's fine. But if you are about to destroy it in a bad meaning, then we may intervene.

I don't know if something like *The War of the Worlds* by H.G. Wells will ever happen, but we wouldn't be so easily attacked and destroyed by a virus. Humans are the ones attacked by viruses.

A

I see. You have such deep love.

YAIDRON

I am a kind person.

A

I have spoken with you during spiritual message

recordings that haven't been released to the public as well, and my conclusion is that you are truly a loving person. Right now, people see you expressing yourself through only a portion of your forms, so you're probably just wrapped in too much mystery. Also, the word "reptilian" alone… I'm sure that doesn't cover everything about you, though.

YAIDRON

No. It's because it's impossible for you to understand unless I say that I am a space person from somewhere in the universe.

A

It's impossible. You take a particular form and say various things depending on the work you are doing at that time, but I have realized that people are apt to make mistakes if they make judgments based solely on that.

YAIDRON

When you study abroad in another country, you will gain a wider perspective. But if you were to be instantly transported alive to another planet and then lived there for a while before returning home, it would very likely be quite difficult for you to describe the experience. Because you would be like Urashima Taro[10].

6
A Message for Earthlings

It is necessary to nurture people who follow the words of the Lord

A
Do you have any messages for us here at the end as a summary?

YAIDRON
Hmm... El Cantare has descended. I think this means that Earthlings need to attract a brighter future even more. But from now, you might see a world in which the people will instead seem to regress due to the coming collapse and chaos that will last for a while. That period may be tough, but through it, you need to nurture people who follow the words of the Lord. It's no good if all that appear are large numbers of people who make judgments based on pretentious intellect and their own sense of right and wrong. Many such people can be seen within Happy Science staff members and

believers too. Briefly put, I get the feeling that there are quite a few people who believe the teachings as long as they benefit in this life, such as assisting them in their work, helping them advance in their career, but don't listen otherwise. I guess it can't be helped. I feel that one of my tasks is to relieve El Cantare's loneliness and support him until the end.

A
Uh-huh.

YAIDRON
We are aware that you are at that level, so please do not be in despair over the state of humanity.

"God is actually a great mass of enlightenment"

A
After all, your message is the same key phrase as yesterday, "With Savior." Perhaps you are saying that we must be more determined to walk together with El Cantare.

YAIDRON

Right. However, as long as you dwell within physical bodies, there is a certain amount of resistance, like when swimming through water. In that sense, this is a precious opportunity that will enable you to train and improve the entity called the mind.

A

I see.

YAIDRON

Having a physical body comes with a weak point—you are susceptible to losing your way and being unable to see the truth, but it is because you are exploring your mind while in a physical body that you are capable of training your mind. And training your mind leads you to enlightenment. Enlightenment is actually an important force you need to survive throughout the universe, and God is actually a great mass of enlightenment.

A

So, after all, dwelling in a physical body as an Earthling is an advantage, considering Earth is a training ground.

YAIDRON

You should take that into consideration. It does no good to practice swimming on the floor. You can only master swimming by actually practicing in a pool or at the beach. No matter how much you practice it on the floor, it doesn't amount to actual swimming practice. Reading about how to swim won't be enough, either. In the end, you have to actually experience it.

It is extremely valuable to come to understand, by dwelling within a physical body, that your true self is your mind, which is separate from your physical body. Those who cannot understand that have become materialists.

A

I understand.

YAIDRON

And those materialists believe that they are smart and clever. This is the cause of confusion in the modern age.

A

Right.

Humans must be guided little by little, with patience

A

Thank you very much for yesterday and today.

YAIDRON

I may have sounded very pessimistic, but sometimes, I can be in a good mood. I pray that such a time comes.

A

Me too.

YAIDRON

I have told you many things over these two or three years, but I feel like my efforts are in vain.

A

You must be feeling so.

YAIDRON

It's not like everyone will start believing if we appear more often. Right now, we have no choice but to gradually make people grow familiar with us by showing ourselves little by little among other religious phenomena.

A

We would like to express our heartfelt gratitude to you for always supporting us in sort of a behind-the-scenes role.

C

Thank you very much.

YAIDRON

On a stuffed panda, the white part would be you, and the black part would be me.

A

No, please don't say that. Thank you so much for helping us behind the scenes. You are much more loving than I am.

YAIDRON

No, no. But you are a very simple, straightforward, hot-tempered type of person who gets in a bad mood easily.

A

[*Laughs.*]

YAIDRON

For us, your simplicity is pretty convenient. When you agree with us in a simple manner, we can work together well. And when you are angry, all I have to do is stay away.

A

[*Laughs.*]

YAIDRON

It's definitely convenient. In some ways, it's harder to deal with those who have more complex thoughts.

A

Because they pretentiously try to do things or try to use you for their own benefit?

YAIDRON
Right.

A
That is not good.

YAIDRON
But I think that humans as a whole must be guided little by little, with patience. There is no other way but to do it tenaciously. [*Sighs.*] It can't be helped.

Some preparations must be made during the age of coronavirus

YAIDRON
As Master meditates in seclusion and listens to the voice of the universe, he may truly become God Himself. Although it is sad for the disciples to see the gap ever widening between them and Him, it can't be helped. You must not steal the Savior's time.

A

Right. I get the feeling that we disciples need to accept the fact that we will gradually become even more distant from Master in the future.

YAIDRON

Even Jesus, after giving lectures and performing miracles surrounded by thousands of people, crossed over a lake and secluded himself up in the mountains. It's because, unless he was alone, he couldn't keep his true mind or speak with us. Some type of seclusion is important. Appearing is also important, though.

Some kind of preparation must be made during the age of coronavirus. In other words, during this period, you should do things that you ordinarily wouldn't be able to. It might be a good time to search for information about the universe.

A

I see. Next year (2021), we will finally release the movie, The Laws of the Universe-Part II.

YAIDRON

Right. If you can raise the level of what everyone thinks is common knowledge, we will be able to reveal many more things.

A

Right. Please continue to... How should I put this? You might want to give up on us, but please continue to watch over us.

YAIDRON

Yes. If this world becomes too difficult to deal with, I will recruit space people members. I will create a group called the Happy Science Space Society.

A

I see. That's wonderful.

YAIDRON

Yes, because it wouldn't only be Earthlings.

A

I think that Master will probably gradually move from his nature as the God of the Earth toward his nature as the God of the Universe.

YAIDRON

But in that case, there will come a time when you have to make enemies of every so-called intellectual on Earth, not just in Japan but in the entire world.

A

I see.

YAIDRON

That is the difficult part. They cannot reach the Truth through the academics of this world.

A

It's unreachable.

YAIDRON

This period of using expedients may continue, but as for how often to appear and when to call the job done, we, advisors from space, are thinking about all that.

A

Right. I understand.

YAIDRON

OK. That's all.

INTERVIEWERS

Thank you very much.

ENDNOTES

1 Metatron is a space being that supports Happy Science and one of the gods of light and is a part of Jesus Christ's space soul (Amor). See Part II, Chapter One of *Spiritual Reading of Novel Coronavirus Infection Originated in China* (Tokyo: HS Press, 2020).

2 *Painted Skin* is a short story included in *Strange Tales from a Chinese Studio*, a collection of classical Chinese mysterious tales by Pu Songling during the Qing dynasty. The story depicts a specter who wears human skin and turns into a beautiful woman. Happy Science will release a film, *Utsukushiki-Yuwaku—Gendai-no-"Gahi"* (Literally, "Beautiful Temptation: The Modern 'Painted Skin'") (Executive producer and original story by Ryuho Okawa) in Japan, in 2021.

3 R. A. Goal is one of the space beings who are supporting Happy Science. He is one of the commanders of the space defense force and a certified Messiah. See Part II, Chapter Two of aforementioned *Spiritual Reading of Novel Coronavirus Infection Originated in China*.

4 *Honyaku Konnyaku* is a magical food that enables foreign languages to be understood when eaten; One of Doraemon's (a character in a Japanese manga series) secret tools.

5 En no Ozunu is a shaman who lived around the 7th century Japan.

6 Lord Heem is the supreme deity of Vega who is connected to the core consciousness of El Cantare. He said in His spiritual message that "I am a hidden being," and "The idea of Earthlings does not reach me." See the spiritual message held on November 12, 2018, entitled, "A Spiritual Message from the Central God of Vega, Heem" available at all Happy Science locations.

7 Anima is the soul of living things. In the "UFO Reading" (Mr. R 2, Yaidron 4, Planet Indole in Delphinus) recorded on October 21, 2018, Yaidron said he has "Anima Saving" in which he can accumulate anima and use that as the source of the energy to live.

8 Kusatsu is an area in Japan that is famous for hot spring resorts.

9 Dongting Lake Niangniang is a goddess of Lake Dongting, China's second largest freshwater lake in northern Hunan Province. The author recorded "The Prelude to Collapsing the Great Chinese Empire—Spiritual Messages from Deng Xiaoping / the Guardian Spirit of Xi Jinping and Dongting Lake Niangniang [1] [2]—" and "The Beginning of the End of the Communist Party of China—Spiritual Messages from Mao Zedong and Dongting Lake Niangniang [3]—" recorded on July 14, July 16, and July 19, 2020 respectively. These sessions are available for view at all Happy Science temples and branches worldwide.

10 Urashima Taro is a character in Japanese folklore. Taro is taken to the Dragon Palace under the sea by a turtle he rescues, and is welcomed with great joy. He is believed to have spent three years at the palace, but discovers that he had gone for 300 years when he returns to his home town.

Afterword

For almost 40 years now, I have been in an intellectual battle with the mysterious world. From spirits in the highest level of Earth Spirit Group to the deepest level of hell, I have conversed with several thousands of them over time. About 10 years ago, I started conveying the thoughts of space beings. All of this must be unbelievable to people who are living in ignorance.

I myself am intelligent, rational, and have scientific ways of thinking. Since the publication of my early books (such as *The Laws of the Sun*), I've taught about the existence of space beings, about how they have been coming to the Earth since the past civilizations, and also about how there are descendants of space people and space people-Earthling hybrids that are living in today's society among you.

This book discloses the mission of Ryuho Okawa from the perspective of space beings. It also outlines the conditions on how humanity can interact with their space friends who have evolved to the highest level. Everything that is written in this book is fact itself. How I communicate with space beings uses almost the same system as when I conduct spiritual messages.

Ryuho Okawa
Master & CEO of Happy Science Group
August 30, 2020

ABOUT THE AUTHOR

RYUHO OKAWA was born on July 7th 1956, in Tokushima, Japan. After graduating from the University of Tokyo with a law degree, he joined a Tokyo-based trading house. While working at its New York headquarters, he studied international finance at the Graduate Center of the City University of New York. In 1981, he attained Great Enlightenment and became aware that he is El Cantare with a mission to bring salvation to all humankind. In 1986, he established Happy Science. It now has members in over 120 countries across the world, with more than 700 local branches and temples as well as 10,000 missionary houses around the world. The total number of lectures has exceeded 3,200 (of which more than 150 are in English) and over 2,700 books (of which more than 550 are Spiritual Interview Series) have been published, many of which are translated into 31 languages. Many of the books, including *The Laws of the Sun* have become best sellers or million sellers. To date, Happy Science has produced 20 movies. The original story and original concept were given by the Executive Producer Ryuho Okawa. Recent movie titles are *The Real Exorcist* (live-action, May 2020), *Living in the Age of Miracles* (documentary, Aug. 2020), and *Twiceborn* (live-action, scheduled to be released in Oct. 2020). He has also composed the lyrics and music of over 150 songs, such as theme songs and featured songs of movies. Moreover, he is the Founder of Happy Science University and Happy Science Academy (Junior and Senior High School), Founder and President of the Happiness Realization Party, Founder and Honorary Headmaster of Happy Science Institute of Government and Management, Founder of IRH Press Co., Ltd., and the Chairperson of New Star Production Co., Ltd. and ARI Production Co., Ltd.

WHAT IS EL CANTARE?

El Cantare means "the Light of the Earth," and is the Supreme God of the Earth who has been guiding humankind since the beginning of Genesis. He is whom Jesus called Father and Muhammad called Allah. Different parts of El Cantare's core consciousness have descended to Earth in the past, once as Alpha and another as Elohim. His branch spirits, such as Shakyamuni Buddha and Hermes, have descended to Earth many times and helped to flourish many civilizations. To unite various religions and to integrate various fields of study in order to build a new civilization on Earth, a part of the core consciousness has descended to Earth as Master Ryuho Okawa.

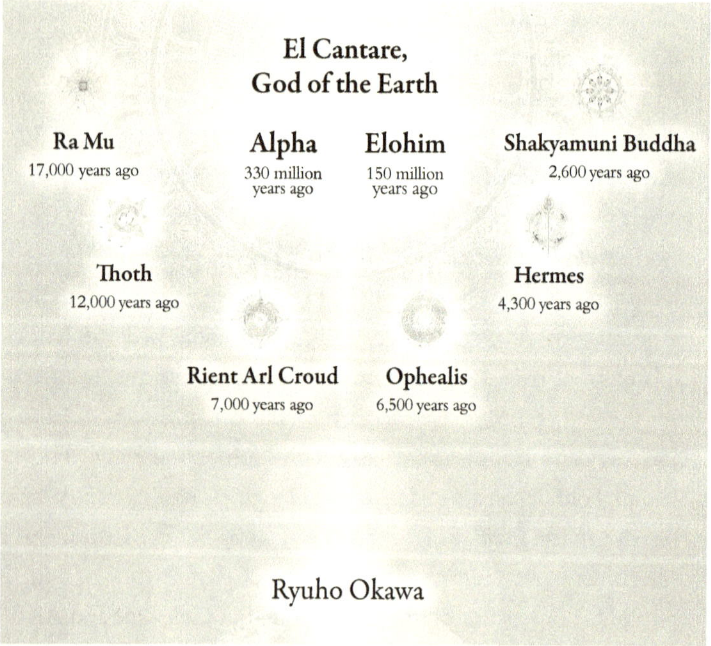

Alpha is a part of the core consciousness of El Cantare who descended to Earth around 330 million years ago. Alpha preached Earth's Truths to harmonize and unify Earth-born humans and space people who came from other planets.

Elohim is a part of El Cantare's core consciousness who descended to Earth around 150 million years ago. He gave wisdom, mainly on the differences of light and darkness, good and evil.

Shakyamuni Buddha was born as a prince into the Shakya Clan in India around 2,600 years ago. When he was 29 years old, he renounced the world and sought enlightenment. He later attained Great Enlightenment and founded Buddhism.

Hermes is one of the 12 Olympian gods in Greek mythology, but the spiritual Truth is that he taught the teachings of love and progress around 4,300 years ago that became the origin of the current Western civilization. He is a hero that truly existed.

Ophealis was born in Greece around 6,500 years ago and was the leader who took an expedition to as far as Egypt. He is the God of miracles, prosperity, and arts, and is known as Osiris in the Egyptian mythology.

Rient Arl Croud was born as a king of the ancient Incan Empire around 7,000 years ago and taught about the mysteries of the mind. In the heavenly world, he is responsible for the interactions that take place between various planets.

Thoth was an almighty leader who built the golden age of the Atlantic civilization around 12,000 years ago. In the Egyptian mythology, he is known as god Thoth.

Ra Mu was a leader who built the golden age of the civilization of Mu around 17,000 years ago. As a religious leader and a politician, he ruled by uniting religion and politics.

WHAT IS A SPIRITUAL MESSAGE?

We are all spiritual beings living on this earth. The following is the mechanism behind Master Ryuho Okawa's spiritual messages.

1 You are a spirit

People are born into this world to gain wisdom through various experiences and return to the other world when their lives end. We are all spirits and repeat this cycle in order to refine our souls.

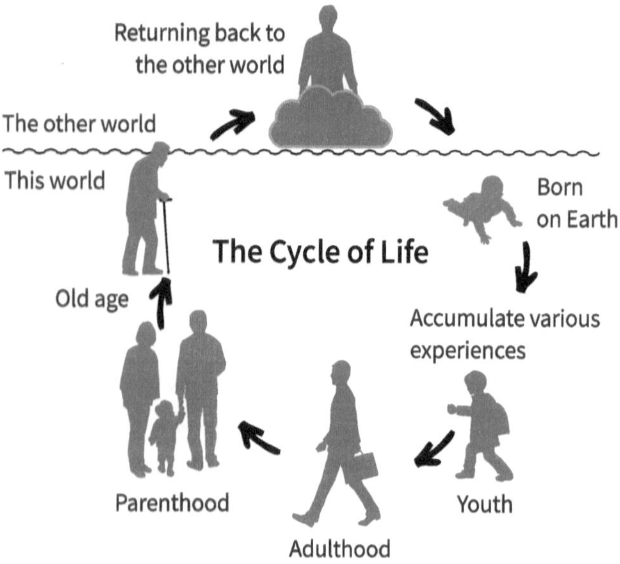

2 You have a guardian spirit

Guardian spirits are those who protect the people who are living on this earth. Each of us has a guardian spirit that watches over us and guides us from the other world. They were us in our past life, and are identical in how we think.

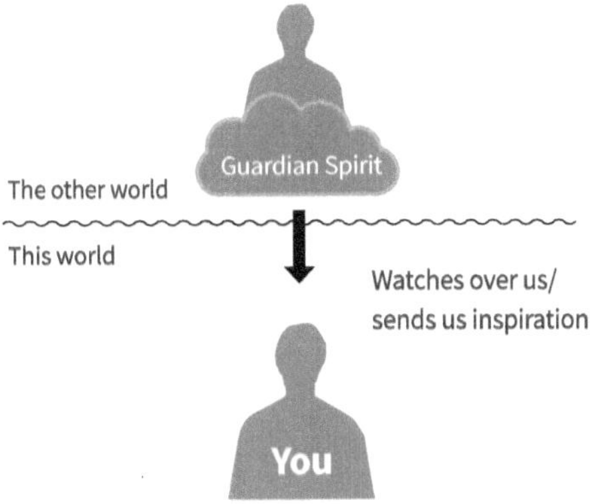

3 How spiritual messages work

Master Ryuho Okawa, through his enlightenment, is capable of summoning any spirit from anywhere in the world, including the spirit world.

Master Okawa's way of receiving spiritual messages is fundamentally different from that of other psychic mediums who undergo trances and are thereby completely taken over by the spirits they are channeling.

Master Okawa's attainment of a high level of enlightenment enables him to retain full control of his consciousness and body throughout the duration of the spiritual message. To allow the spirits to express their own thoughts and personalities freely, however, Master Okawa usually softens the dominancy of his consciousness. This way, he is able to keep his own philosophies out of the way and ensure that the spiritual messages are pure expressions of the spirits he is channeling.

Since guardian spirits think at the same subconscious level as the person living on earth, Master Okawa can summon the spirit and find out what the person on earth is actually thinking. If the person has already returned to the other world, the spirit can give messages to the people living on earth through Master Okawa.

Since 2009, more than 1,100 sessions of spiritual messages have been openly recorded by Master Okawa, and the majority of these have been published. Spiritual messages from the guardian spirits of people living today such as Donald Trump, former Japanese Prime Minister Shinzo Abe and Chinese President Xi Jinping, as well as spiritual messages sent from the spirit world by Jesus Christ, Muhammad, Thomas Edison, Mother Teresa, Steve Jobs and Nelson Mandela are just a tiny pack of spiritual messages that were published so far.

Domestically, in Japan, these spiritual messages are being read by a wide range of politicians and mass media, and the high-level contents of these books are delivering an impact even more on politics, news and public opinion. In recent years, there have been spiritual messages recorded in English, and English translations are being done on the spiritual messages given in Japanese. These have been published overseas, one after another, and have started to shake the world.

For more about spiritual messages and a complete list of books in the Spiritual Interview Series, visit ***okawabooks.com***

ABOUT HAPPY SCIENCE

Happy Science is a global movement that empowers individuals to find purpose and spiritual happiness and to share that happiness with their families, societies, and the world. With more than 12 million members around the world, Happy Science aims to increase awareness of spiritual truths and expand our capacity for love, compassion, and joy so that together we can create the kind of world we all wish to live in.

Activities at Happy Science are based on the Principles of Happiness (Love, Wisdom, Self-Reflection, and Progress). These principles embrace worldwide philosophies and beliefs, transcending boundaries of culture and religions.

Love teaches us to give ourselves freely without expecting anything in return; it encompasses giving, nurturing, and forgiving.

Wisdom leads us to the insights of spiritual truths, and opens us to the true meaning of life and the will of God (the universe, the highest power, Buddha).

Self-Reflection brings a mindful, nonjudgmental lens to our thoughts and actions to help us find our truest selves—the essence of our souls—and deepen our connection to the highest power. It helps us attain a clean and peaceful mind and leads us to the right life path.

Progress emphasizes the positive, dynamic aspects of our spiritual growth—actions we can take to manifest and spread happiness around the world. It's a path that not only expands our soul growth, but also furthers the collective potential of the world we live in.

PROGRAMS AND EVENTS

The doors of Happy Science are open to all. We offer a variety of programs and events, including self-exploration and self-growth programs, spiritual seminars, meditation and contemplation sessions, study groups, and book events.

Our programs are designed to:
* Deepen your understanding of your purpose and meaning in life
* Improve your relationships and increase your capacity to love unconditionally
* Attain peace of mind, decrease anxiety and stress, and feel positive
* Gain deeper insights and a broader perspective on the world
* Learn how to overcome life's challenges

... and much more.

For more information, visit ***happy-science.org****.*

OUR ACTIVITIES

Happy Science does other various activities to provide support for those in need.

- **You Are An Angel! General Incorporated Association**

  Happy Science has a volunteer network in Japan that encourages and supports children with disabilities as well as their parents and guardians.

- **Never Mind School for Truancy**

  At 'Never Mind,' we support students who find it very challenging to attend schools in Japan. We also nurture their self-help spirit and power to rebound against obstacles in life based on Master Okawa's teachings and faith.

- **"Prevention Against Suicide" Campaign since 2003**

  A nationwide campaign to reduce suicides; over 20,000 people commit suicide every year in Japan. "The Suicide Prevention Website-Words of Truth for You-" presents spiritual prescriptions for worries such as depression, lost love, extramarital affairs, bullying and work-related problems, thereby saving many lives.

- **Support for Anti-bullying Campaigns**

  Happy Science provides support for a group of parents and guardians, Network to Protect Children from Bullying, a general incorporated foundation launched in Japan to end bullying, including those that can even be called a criminal offense. So far, the network received more than 5,000 cases and resolved 90% of them.

◆ **The Golden Age Scholarship**

This scholarship is granted to students who can contribute greatly and bring a hopeful future to the world.

◆ **Success No.1**
Buddha's Truth Afterschool Academy

Happy Science has over 180 classrooms throughout Japan and in several cities around the world that focus on afterschool education for children. The education focuses on faith and morals in addition to supporting children's school studies.

◆ **Angel Plan V**

For children under the age of kindergarten, Happy Science holds classes for nurturing healthy, positive, and creative boys and girls.

◆ **Future Stars Training Department**

The Future Stars Training Department was founded within the Happy Science Media Division with the goal of nurturing talented individuals to become successful in the performing arts and entertainment industry.

◆ **New Star Production Co., Ltd.**
ARI Production Co., Ltd.

We have companies to nurture actors and actresses, artists, and vocalists. They are also involved in film production.

DOCUMENTARY MOVIE
HEART TO HEART

In this documentary movie, Happy Science University students visit these NPO activities to discover what salvation truly is, and on the meaning of life, through heart-to-heart interviews.

ABOUT HAPPY SCIENCE MOVIES

TWICEBORN

Coming to Theaters Fall 2020

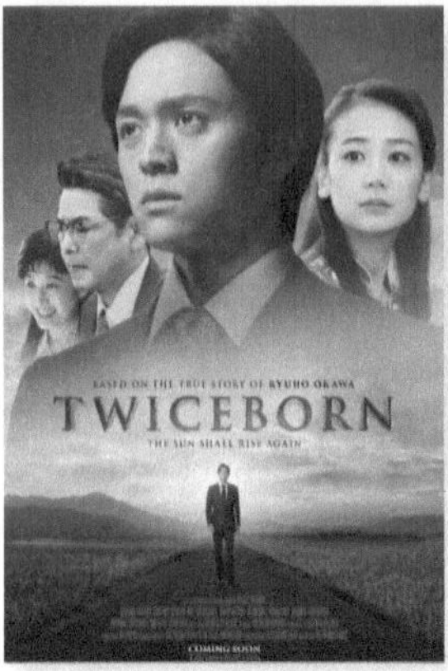

STORY Satoru Ichijo receives a message from the spiritual world and realizes his mission is to lead humankind to happiness. He became a successful businessman while publishing spiritual messages secretly, but the devil's temptation shakes his mind and...

19 Awards from 4 Countries!

OFF COMPETITION 2020 RAINDANCE FILM FESTIVAL SPECIAL SCREENING

WINNER BEST FOREIGN LANGUAGE FEATURE FILM MADRID 2020

OFFICIAL SELECTION SAN DIEGO INTERNATIONAL FILM FESTIVAL

For more information, visit ***www.twicebornmovie.com***

LIVING IN THE AGE OF MIRACLES

A documentary film released in Aug. 2020

An inspirational documentary about two Japanese actors meeting people who experienced miracles in their lives. Through their quest, they find the key to working miracles and learn what "living in the age of miracles" truly means.

6 Awards from USA!

WINNER AWARD OF MERIT SPECIAL MENTION IMPACT DOCS AWARDS

GOLD AWARD Documentary Feature International Independent Film Awards Spring 2020

GOLD AWARD Concept International Independent Film Awards Spring 2020

...and more!

CONTACT INFORMATION

Happy Science is a worldwide organization with faith centers around the globe. For a comprehensive list of centers, visit the worldwide directory at *happy-science.org*. The following are some of the many Happy Science locations:

UNITED STATES AND CANADA

New York
79 Franklin St., New York, NY 10013
Phone: 212-343-7972
Fax: 212-343-7973
Email: ny@happy-science.org
Website: happyscience-na.org

New Jersey
725 River Rd, #102B, Edgewater, NJ 07020
Phone: 201-313-0127
Fax: 201-313-0120
Email: nj@happy-science.org
Website: happyscience-na.org

Florida
5208 8th St., St. Zephyrhills, FL 33542
Phone: 813-715-0000
Fax: 813-715-0010
Email: florida@happy-science.org
Website: happyscience-na.org

Atlanta
1874 Piedmont Ave., NE Suite 360-C
Atlanta, GA 30324
Phone: 404-892-7770
Email: atlanta@happy-science.org
Website: happyscience-na.org

San Francisco
525 Clinton St.
Redwood City, CA 94062
Phone & Fax: 650-363-2777
Email: sf@happy-science.org
Website: happyscience-na.org

Los Angeles
1590 E. Del Mar Blvd., Pasadena, CA 91106
Phone: 626-395-7775
Fax: 626-395-7776
Email: la@happy-science.org
Website: happyscience-na.org

Orange County
10231 Slater Ave., #204
Fountain Valley, CA 92708
Phone: 714-745-1140
Email: oc@happy-science.org
Website: happyscience-na.org

San Diego
7841 Balboa Ave., Suite #202
San Diego, CA 92111
Phone: 626-395-7775
Fax: 626-395-7776
E-mail: sandiego@happy-science.org
Website: happyscience-na.org

Hawaii
Phone: 808-591-9772
Fax: 808-591-9776
Email: hi@happy-science.org
Website: happyscience-na.org

Kauai
3343 Kanakolu Street, Suite 5
Lihue, HI 96766, U.S.A.
Phone: 808-822-7007
Fax: 808-822-6007
Email: kauai-hi@happy-science.org
Website: kauai.happyscience-na.org

Toronto
845 The Queensway
Etobicoke ON M8Z 1N6 Canada
Phone: 1-416-901-3747
Email: toronto@happy-science.org
Website: happy-science.ca

Vancouver
#201-2607 East 49th Avenue
Vancouver, BC, V5S 1J9, Canada
Phone: 1-604-437-7735
Fax: 1-604-437-7764
Email: vancouver@happy-science.org
Website: happy-science.ca

INTERNATIONAL

Tokyo
1-6-7 Togoshi, Shinagawa
Tokyo, 142-0041 Japan
Phone: 81-3-6384-5770
Fax: 81-3-6384-5776
Email: tokyo@happy-science.org
Website: happy-science.org

Seoul
74, Sadang-ro 27-gil,
Dongjak-gu, Seoul, Korea
Phone: 82-2-3478-8777
Fax: 82-2-3478-9777
Email: korea@happy-science.org
Website: happyscience-korea.org

London
3 Margaret St.
London,W1W 8RE United Kingdom
Phone: 44-20-7323-9255
Fax: 44-20-7323-9344
Email: eu@happy-science.org
Website: happyscience-uk.org

Taipei
No. 89, Lane 155, Dunhua N. Road
Songshan District, Taipei City 105, Taiwan
Phone: 886-2-2719-9377
Fax: 886-2-2719-5570
Email: taiwan@happy-science.org
Website: happyscience-tw.org

Sydney
516 Pacific Hwy, Lane Cove North,
NSW 2066, Australia
Phone: 61-2-9411-2877
Fax: 61-2-9411-2822
Email: sydney@happy-science.org

Malaysia
No 22A, Block 2, Jalil Link Jalan Jalil Jaya 2,
Bukit Jalil 57000, Kuala Lumpur, Malaysia
Phone: 60-3-8998-7877
Fax: 60-3-8998-7977
Email: malaysia@happy-science.org
Website: happyscience.org.my

Brazil Headquarters
Rua. Domingos de Morais 1154,
Vila Mariana, Sao Paulo SP
CEP 04009-002, Brazil
Phone: 55-11-5088-3800
Fax: 55-11-5088-3806
Email: sp@happy-science.org
Website: happyscience.com.br

Nepal
Kathmandu Metropolitan City Ward
No. 15,
Ring Road, Kimdol,
Sitapaila Kathmandu, Nepal
Phone: 97-714-272931
Email: nepal@happy-science.org

Jundiai
Rua Congo, 447, Jd. Bonfiglioli
Jundiai-CEP, 13207-340
Phone: 55-11-4587-5952
Email: jundiai@happy-science.org

Uganda
Plot 877 Rubaga Road, Kampala
P.O. Box 34130, Kampala, Uganda
Phone: 256-79-4682-121
Email: uganda@happy-science.org
Website: happyscience-uganda.org

ABOUT HAPPINESS REALIZATION PARTY

The Happiness Realization Party (HRP) was founded in May 2009 by Master Ryuho Okawa as part of the Happy Science Group to offer concrete and proactive solutions to the current issues such as military threats from North Korea and China and the long-term economic recession. HRP aims to implement drastic reforms of the Japanese government, thereby bringing peace and prosperity to Japan. To accomplish this, HRP proposes two key policies:

1) Strengthening the national security and the Japan-U.S. alliance, which plays a vital role in the stability of Asia.

2) Improving the Japanese economy by implementing drastic tax cuts, taking monetary easing measures and creating new major industries.

HRP advocates that Japan should offer a model of a religious nation that allows diverse values and beliefs to coexist, and that contributes to global peace.

For more information, visit ***en.hr-party.jp***

ABOUT IRH PRESS USA

IRH Press USA Inc. was founded in 2013 as an affiliated firm of IRH Press Co., Ltd. Based in New York, the press publishes books in various categories including spirituality, religion, and self-improvement and publishes books by Ryuho Okawa, the author of over 100 million books sold worldwide. For more information, visit okawabooks.com.

Follow us on:

Facebook: Okawa Books
Twitter: Okawa Books
Goodreads: Ryuho Okawa
Instagram: OkawaBooks
Pinterest: Okawa Books

MEDIA

OKAWA BOOK CLUB

A conversation about Ryuho Okawa's titles, topics ranging from self-help, current affairs, spirituality and religions.

Available at iTunes, Spotify and Amazon Music.

Apple iTunes:
https://podcasts.apple.com/us/podcast/okawa-book-club/id1527893043

Spotify:
https://open.spotify.com/show/09mpgX2iJ6stVm4eBRdo2b

Amazon Music:
https://music.amazon.com/podcasts/7b759f24-ff72-4523-bfee-24f48294998f/Okawa-Book-Club

BOOKS BY RYUHO OKAWA

RYUHO OKAWA'S LAWS SERIES

The Laws Series is an annual volume of books that are mainly comprised of Ryuho Okawa's lectures on various topics that highlight principles and guidelines for the activities of Happy Science every year. *The Laws of the Sun*, the first publication of the laws series, ranked in the annual best-selling list in Japan in 1987. Since then, all of the laws series' titles have ranked in the annual best-selling list for more than two decades, setting socio-cultural trends in Japan and around the world.

The 26th Laws Series

THE LAWS OF STEEL

LIVING A LIFE OF RESILIENCE, CONFIDENCE AND PROSPERITY

Paperback • 256 pages • $16.95
ISBN: 978-1-942125-65-5

This book is a compilation of six lectures that Ryuho Okawa gave in 2018 and 2019, each containing passionate messages for us to open a brighter future. This powerful and inspiring book will not only show us the ways to achieve true happiness and prosperity, but also the ways to solve many global issues we now face. It presents us with wisdom that is based on a spiritual perspective, and a new design for our future society. Through this book, we can overcome differences in values and create a peaceful world, thereby ushering in a Golden Age.

THE TRILOGY

The first three volumes of the Laws Series, *The Laws of the Sun*, *The Golden Laws*, and *The Nine Dimensions* make a trilogy that completes the basic framework of the teachings of God's Truths. *The Laws of the Sun* discusses the structure of God's Laws, *The Golden Laws* expounds on the doctrine of time, and *The Nine Dimensions* reveals the nature of space.

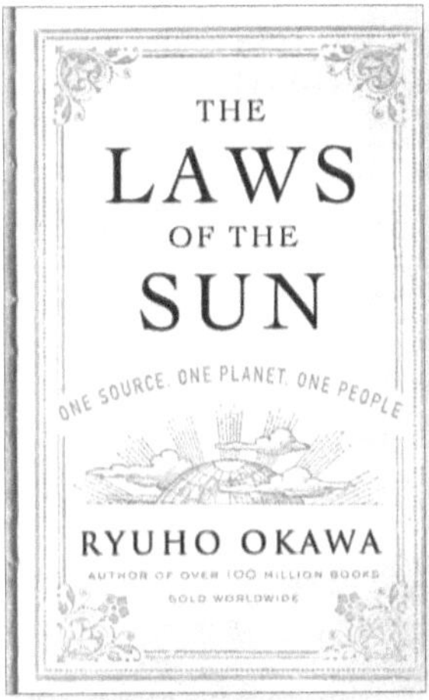

THE LAWS OF THE SUN

ONE SOURCE, ONE PLANET, ONE PEOPLE

Paperback • 288 pages • $15.95
ISBN: 978-1-942125-43-3

IMAGINE IF YOU COULD ASK GOD why He created this world and what spiritual laws He used to shape us—and everything around us. If we could understand His designs and intentions, we could discover what our goals in life should be and whether our actions move us closer to those goals or farther away.

At a young age, a spiritual calling prompted Ryuho Okawa to outline what he innately understood to be universal truths for all humankind. In *The Laws of the Sun*, Okawa outlines these laws of the universe and provides a road map for living one's life with greater purpose and meaning.

In this powerful book, Ryuho Okawa reveals the transcendent nature of consciousness and the secrets of our multidimensional universe and our place in it. By understanding the different stages of love and following the Buddhist Eightfold Path, he believes we can speed up our eternal process of development. *The Laws of the Sun* shows the way to realize true happiness—a happiness that continues from this world through the other.

For a complete list of books, visit ***okawabooks.com***

THE GOLDEN LAWS

HISTORY THROUGH THE EYES OF THE ETERNAL BUDDHA

Paperback • 201 pages • $14.95
ISBN: 978-1-941779-81-1

Throughout history, Great Guiding Spirits of Light have been present on Earth in both the East and the West at crucial points in human history to further our spiritual development. *The Golden Laws* reveals how Divine Plan has been unfolding on Earth, and outlines 5,000 years of the secret history of humankind. Once we understand the true course of history, through past, present and into the future, we cannot help but become aware of the significance of our spiritual mission in the present age.

THE NINE DIMENSIONS

UNVEILING THE LAWS OF ETERNITY

Paperback • 168 pages • $15.95
ISBN: 978-0-982698-56-3

This book is a window into the mind of our loving God, who designed this world and the vast, wondrous world of our afterlife as a school with many levels through which our souls learn and grow. When the religions and cultures of the world discover the truth of their common spiritual origin, they will be inspired to accept their differences, come together under faith in God, and build an era of harmony and peaceful progress on Earth.

NEW TITLE

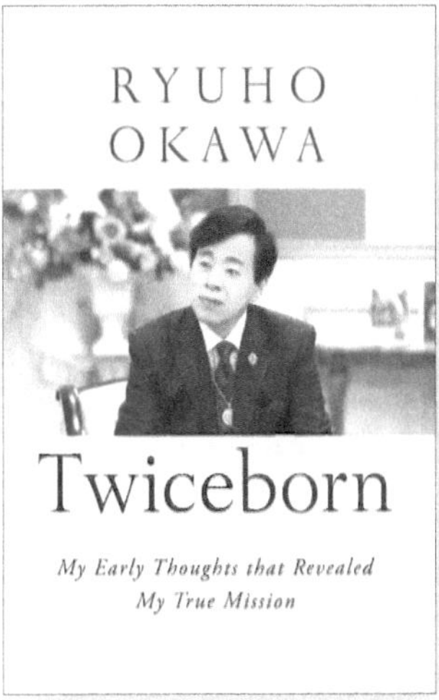

TWICEBORN

MY EARLY THOUGHTS THAT REVEALED MY TRUE MISSION

Paperback • 206 pages • $19.95
ISBN: 978-1-942125-74-7

This semi-autobiography of Ryuho Okawa reveals the origins of his thoughts and how he made up his mind to establish Happy Science to spread the Truth to the world. It also contains the very first grand lecture where he declared himself as El Cantare. The timeless wisdom in *Twiceborn* will surely inspire you and help you fulfill your mission in this lifetime.

THE NEW RESURRECTION

MY MIRACULOUS STORY OF OVERCOMING ILLNESS AND DEATH

Hardcover • 224 pages • $19.95
ISBN: 978-1-942125-64-8

The New Resurrection is an autobiographical account of an astonishing miracle experienced by author Ryuho Okawa in 2004. This event was adapted into the feature-length film *Immortal Hero*, released in Japan, the United States and Canada during the Fall of 2019. Today, Okawa lives each day with the readiness to die for the Truth and has dedicated his life to selflessly guiding faith seekers towards spiritual development and happiness. The appendix showcases a myriad of accomplishments by Okawa, chronicled after his miraculous resurrection.

THE LAWS OF HAPPINESS

LOVE, WISDOM, SELF-REFLECTION AND PROGRESS

Paperback • 264 pages • $16.95
ISBN: 978-1-942125-70-9

This book endeavors to answer the question, "What is true happiness?" This milestone text introduces four distinct principles, based on the "Laws of Mind" and sourced from Okawa's real-world experience, to guide readers towards sustainable happiness. Okawa's four "Principles of Happiness" present an easy, yet profound framework to ground this rapidly advanced and highly competitive society. In practice, Okawa outlines pragmatic steps to revitalize our ambition to lead a happier and meaningful life.

For a complete list of books, visit ***okawabooks.com***

Spiritual Interviews with the Guardian Spirits of Biden and Trump

Paperback • 200 pages • $11.95
ISBN: 978-1-943869-92-3

The 2020 U.S. presidential election will be a turning point in history. In this book, we spiritually closed in on the true thoughts of Biden and Trump to get a forecast of the presidential election. In short, China could become the next hegemonic state if Biden is elected the president. Who you vote for could change people's lives, for better or worse.

The Real Exorcist

Attain Wisdom to Conquer Evil

Paperback • 208 pages • $16.95
ISBN:978-1-942125-67-9

This is a profound spiritual text backed by the author's nearly 40 years of real-life experience with spiritual phenomena. In it, Okawa teaches how we may discern and overcome our negative tendencies, by acquiring the right knowledge, mindset and lifestyle.

SHAKYAMUNI BUDDHA'S FUTURE PREDICTION

Paperback • 213 pages • $13.95
ISBN: 978-1-943869-91-6

In this book, the spirits of Shakyamuni Buddha and John Lennon warn us about the troubles that await humankind, require us who live today to reflect on the arrogance of belittling God, and teach us how to overcome difficulties. What the world needs now are many people who work as a part of God's power. You, too, can become a part of the power to save the world.

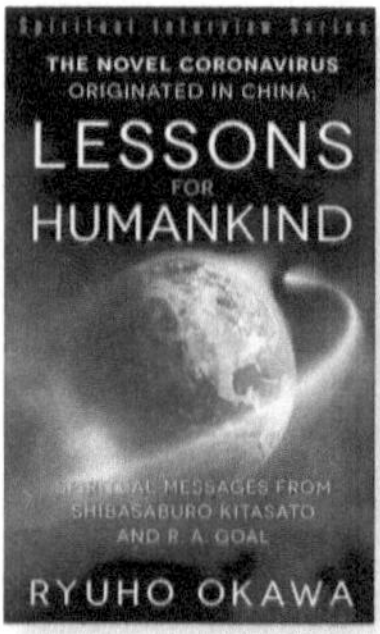

THE NOVEL CORONAVIRUS ORIGINATED IN CHINA: LESSONS FOR HUMANKIND

SPIRITUAL MESSAGES FROM SHIBASABURO KITASATO AND R. A. GOAL

Paperback • 228 pages • $13.95
ISBN: 978-1-943869-88-6

This book records spiritual messages from a bacteriologist and a space being. They disclose many truths about the novel coronavirus pandemic, such as China's hidden secrets, what the future holds, and hopeful messages for humanity. Only when humanity learns what we are to learn from this pandemic, can we escape this worldwide crisis and create a new age.

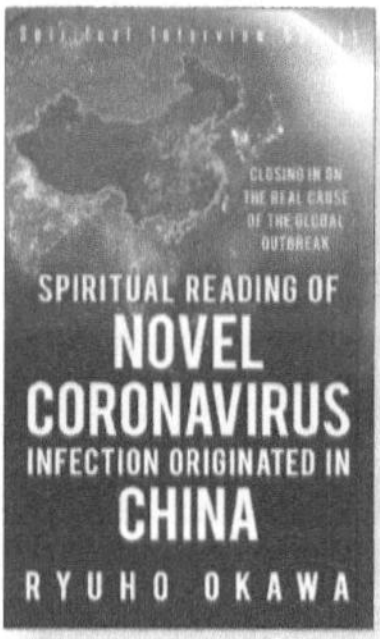

SPIRITUAL READING OF NOVEL CORONAVIRUS INFECTION ORIGINATED IN CHINA

CLOSING IN ON THE REAL CAUSE OF THE GLOBAL OUTBREAK

Paperback • 278 pages • $13.95
ISBN: 978-1-943869-77-0

This worldwide pandemic is not a mere act of nature nor a coincidence, but rather, heaven's warning to humanity, especially China. Through this book, you can find out "the immunity" against the novel coronavirus, among other shocking truths.

For a complete list of books, visit ***okawabooks.com***

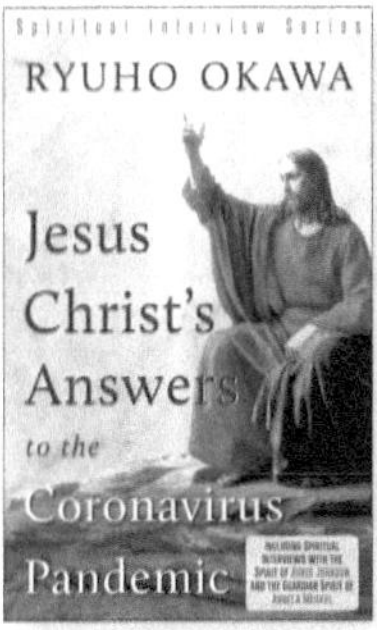

Jesus Christ's Answers to the Coronavirus Pandemic

Paperback • 204 pages • $11.95
ISBN: 978-1-943869-81-7

In this book, the spirit of Jesus answers the causes, prospects, and coping strategies for the novel coronavirus pandemic. Instead of hoping for the development of an effective vaccine to come soon, we should use our spiritual power to defeat the evil thoughts that spiritually possess this virus. It's a book for all who believe in Jesus.

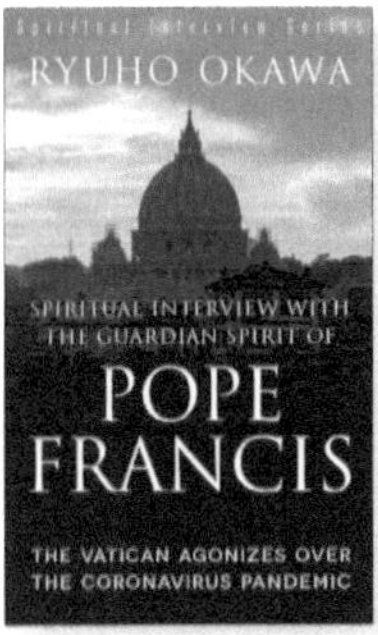

Spiritual Interview with the Guardian Spirit of Pope Francis

The Vatican Agonizes over the Coronavirus Pandemic

Paperback • 268 pages • $13.95
ISBN: 978-1-943869-84-8

In this book, the guardian spirit of Pope Francis confesses his hopelessness, goodwill, and limit as a human being amid the ongoing coronavirus pandemic. Are his prayers heard by Jesus? By also reading *Jesus Christ's Answers to the Coronavirus Pandemic*, you will be able to understand the true will of Jesus and the faith in true God.

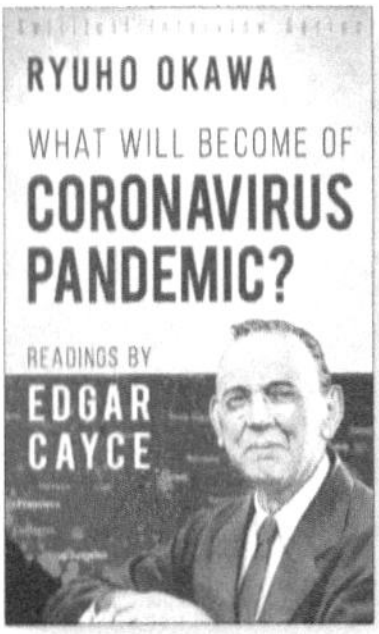

What Will Become of Coronavirus Pandemic?

Readings by Edgar Cayce

Paperback • 86 pages • $9.95
ISBN: 978-1-943869-82-4

Edgar Cayce, now a spirit in heaven, tells us that the novel coronavirus infection is likely to spread even further, but he also teaches us the truth behind it and how to deal with it. But you, yourself, can gain the power to defeat the novel coronavirus. Here is your light of hope.

THE LAWS OF BRONZE
Love One Another, Become One People

UFOS CAUGHT ON CAMERA!
A Spiritual Investigation on Videos and Photos of the Luminous Objects Visiting Earth

ALIEN INVASION
Can We Defend Earth?

CHINA'S SECRET MILITARY BASES
A Remote-Viewing Investigation of Suspicious Satellite Images

THE NEXT GREAT AWAKENING
A Spiritual Renaissance

THE NEW RESURRECTION
My Miraculous Story of Overcoming Illness and Death

THE ROYAL ROAD OF LIFE
Beginning Your Path of Inner Peace, Virtue, and a Life of Purpose

THE HELL YOU NEVER KNEW
And How to Avoid Going There

SPIRITUAL WORLD 101
A Guide to a Spiritually Happy Life

---

*For a complete list of books, visit **okawabooks.com***

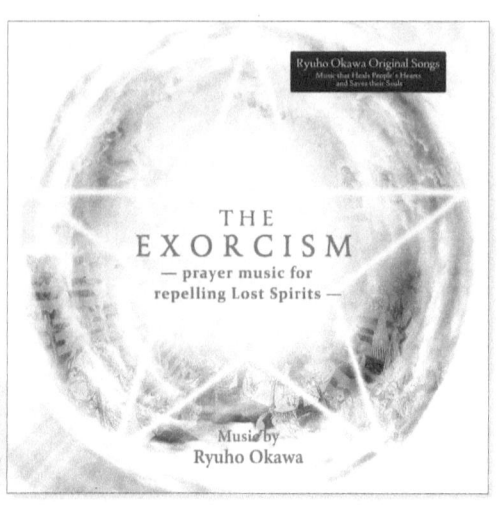